Cracking Calvin

Cracking Calvin

DENNIS R. WILSON

RESOURCE *Publications* • Eugene, Oregon

CRACKING CALVIN

Resource Publications
An Imprint of Wipf and Stock Publishers
199 W. 8th Ave., Suite 3
Eugene, OR 97401

www.wipfandstock.com

PAPERBACK ISBN: 978-1-6667-1180-6
HARDCOVER ISBN: 978-1-6667-1181-3
EBOOK ISBN: 978-1-6667-1182-0

AUGUST 31, 2021

People of Trinity Baptist Church, Priest River, Id

Contents

Chapter 1

The Point of it All

... I most certainly understand now that God is not one to show partiality, but in every nation the man who fears Him and does what is right, is welcome to Him.

—ACTS 10:35 (NASB)

LIFE IS FULL OF little mysteries. Take for example the dimorphism of the sexes as in the worldwide phenomena of women with long hair. And yes, there have been societies where men also wore their hair long, but even in these, women almost always persisted, so it is not just in contrast to men. It is just interesting to me that for no obvious reason there always seems to be a men's and a women's hair length for every human society, and that "look" seems to have been consistent over all people everywhere. So what difference is there in the female that seems to produce this preponderance for long hair? This is all very mysterious to me.

Then there is the universal phenomenon of things known that have no reason to be known; and things done that have no business being done. Why for example did many Portuguese map makers draw in the New World before Columbus had ever been there? And how did the ancient Chinese make pictures of what appear to be dinosaurs on their zodiac wheels? How did the Mayans know the stegosaurus well enough to carve him on the doors of ancient temples? And why did some ancient cultures draw enormous pictographs on the surface of the ground, drawings that could only make sense from thousands of feet in the air? And what possessed the people of Easter Island to carve enormous heads, place them all around the island, and then vanish into the sea?

All over the world there are places where huge irregularly shaped stones have been set into walls, making them look like enormous jigsaw puzzles. Some of these stones are so heavy we would be hard pressed to move them with modern cranes. Yet at Machu Picchu, on a mountain in Peru, there is a wall whose pieces are simply enormous with very irregular shapes. Somehow each stone fits perfectly into the wall, and as they say, you couldn't get a credit card between them. How did ancient cultures do such things?

But perhaps the least considered category is the most fascinating. This is the sort of mystery where something has come into common usage without an easily understood reason to exist. Such is the strange anomaly of the seven day week. The week is practiced by every known culture on the face of the earth and yet there is no apparent reason why a seven day unit of time should exist at all. The week may seem quite ordinary because we all use it all the time, but the seven day week is actually a huge mystery.

The year reflects the orbit of the earth, something even ancient man could have taken note of by the positions of various celestial events and objects. And at about a thirty day interval the moon goes through its phases, at least sketching out the month. But what celestial measurement drives the week? There appears to be none. And seven seems such an arbitrary interval. It doesn't have any natural clock with which to compare it, no orbiting body, no naturally recurring event like Old Faithful blowing its' top every thirty minutes, nothing. It is without obvious cosmological backup, and yet the whole earth uses the seven day week. Though intimately familiar to all of us, this is a real puzzle. One might argue that it reflects the quarter month, but most months do not divide naturally into four week long units, at least not evenly. Christians and Jews who accept the Book of Genesis would say it is the common memory of the Creation Week, as recorded there in Genesis. But that might be hard to prove to the satisfaction of atheists. Could there be some common memory among people of the Biblical seven days of Creation? A Buddhist might not buy into that scenario because the Bible is not that important to his culture. So we ask again, why seven, and why everywhere? It is a huge mystery.

Atheists of the French Revolution, wanting to suppress the Bible, dictated a ten day week trying to wean people away from God. But that seemed to fade out quickly. Nobody even remembers why it vanished but somehow it just went away. And in Russia, during the Communist revolution, workmen were placed on rotating five and then six day work intervals, but it never lasted. By 1940 they had all evolved back to seven days with Sunday as the day of rest. So we ask, why does the Bible's week of Creation, the seven day week, end up being honored by nations of Hindus or Islamists or Communists? Nobody knows.

Then there are the really important questions, such as those about meaning. They can be the most mysterious of all, and yet these are serious issues. Sooner or later every person on earth begins asking such fundamental questions as; "How did I get here, and where am I going"? And, "what is the meaning of life?" Actually everyone wants to know why he was born. And Christians are no different. Questions about life puzzle us too, though we make strong assertions that we do have answers, and sometimes we act like we have all the answers; but we really don't. We do have a Book, or at least we are supposed to have a most unique Book, if we take time to actually read it. And though the Bible may be the most incredible writing on earth, it may also be the most neglected. But it is still the document with the greatest circulation and readership the earth has ever known. And no matter what we call it, the Bible, the Word of God, or even the Holy Scriptures, Christians believe this is a revelation which came directly from the hand of the Lord

God Almighty. And so we actually do believe that if the really important answers can be found anywhere, they must be in this the greatest book known, somewhere.

So it should not be that amazing to discover this book is yet another one of life's truly important mysteries. Actually the Bible is far more amazing than most people know. How could any book become so transcendent in the affairs of men? Oddly enough it applies as well to a stone age tribesman in Indonesia as it does to an executive behind his computer in New York City. It applies just as well to a secretary in Paris, as to a shaman in the mountains of Peru. All nations and tongues on earth find truth in this one book. And it does seem to be the one source equal to the task of answering life's deepest questions.

In fact, after examining the Bible closely, it seems to be a miracle which anyone can hold in his hand! In so many ways it qualifies as something unique on the earth, something outside of human experience. Yet strangely, its' topic is mankind and his relationship to the deity who introduces himself as Creator of the universe. Those who examine it in depth are left wondering how such a thing can even exist.

It is a book, or rather a library, written from the pens of at least forty different authors, on three different continents, in two major and several minor languages, and put together over a period of nearly two thousand years all elements of its construction that ought to render it a cacophony of conflicting voices and ideas. But the Bible fits together as well as those walls we spoke about in Peru. And in every single subset (book) of this library the author claims he came into contact with a being of such towering presence he could only be described as God. A being who inspired him to write what he wrote. Even so, while all this appears to be utterly wonderful, and backed up with many lines of evidence, such claims can only be described as one side of a debate that rages on to this moment. There are others, mostly disbelievers, with very different and lesser points of view. Some would even denigrate the Bible into nothing more than an evolved bit of desert folklore put together from the oral traditions of four basic Bedouin traditions.

We acknowledge such critics but we do not accept their rambling and contradictory theories. Weighed in the balance they are simply spiritual indigestion, for there is ample evidence, even from a cursory examination of its' internal construction, which shows that the Bible is much more than fable and folklore; faith in the Word is not based on empty deception or even ancient tradition and certainly not the evolving religious expressions of desert wanderers.

No, the Bible has a majesty unlike any other written document. In spite of a production time covering two thousand years, and with so many human authors, the Bible emerges a moral, philosophical, theological, historical, scientific and prophetic unity. There is no noise here; just a seamless interconnecting flow that explains the workings of everything. Even at the level of sub-themes, the Bible never stumbles or drops a thread. It picks up sub topics in a different book, sometimes hundreds or even thousands of years and hundreds of miles away, from when the preliminary point was taken, all of it serving to illuminate some major theme it was making in the first place. Careful reading of this book, even down to the single word, always yields far reaching understanding. It maintains an internal unity down to the language it chooses; and has whole sections which begin in one language and finish in another.

Despite being fashioned in Babylon, and Persia, and Syria, and Greece, and Rome, to say nothing of Israel, the Bible is the most self defining, self articulating, book ever written. Not a word on the page seems wasted. One section clarifies and illumines another. And throughout its history, its poetry, its teaching, and its prophecy, while carrying the personality of the human who stroked the pen, the greater personality of a single author emerges; seemingly the Lord God himself.

On top of all that, it can be argued the Bible contains the only legitimate prophecy (the actual telling of the future) in all of human experience. Many books make claims to being prophetic; but only the Bible backs up that claim with hard data that can be examined through archeology, history, and literature. The Bible has accurately predicted many hundreds of events that are already in the past; even sometimes naming the actual names of those who will carry out the prophecy hundreds of years before they were born. Two kings, one Jewish and one Persian, come to mind. They are named by name and shown their mission in life hundreds of years before they were even born. How can that even happen?

With so varied a pedigree mathematicians tell us such a document is a statistical impossibility. There is simply nothing else like it on earth, and frankly it should not exist. No book of great mystery, like that which a Nostradamus or an Edgar Cayce passed on to us, no mathematics book of probability, no book of some other religion, and no analysis of futurity even comes close. Nothing else like it exists anywhere. So it is no wonder many believe the Bible to be the only book capable of passing the test of divine authorship.

And if so it has the potential of answering the greatest questions posed by humanity. If the meaning of life can be known at all, we believe it must be in the Bible. The challenge is to sift through its pages to find the treasure. Parts of this book are so simple a child can grasp what is said, and others so deep the greatest philosophers on earth still grapple with even limited understanding of them.

All of which is to say the Bible can be treated as a kind of story, or actual history, and with a very different outcome to each. A story might make it worth something, say for instruction in living, nice to have but not necessity. Real history would make it reality. And my argument is that the overwhelming preponderance of evidence does make it history, except in those locations where it describes itself as narrative or poetry. Is the Bible an allegory of the sort which is Bunyan's "Pilgrim's Progress"? Or is the Bible the actual story of man? The evidence describes a book of extreme reality like nothing before it; the Book of Man by the author of Man.

And since it is a book, like every other book, it makes sense to begin such a search with the beginning. If we can find the meaning to life at all, we think it must be near the beginning of the Bible where it presents an explanation of how man was first created. Perhaps hidden among the foundations upon which the world rests lie clues as to why we exist. And in finding the reason for our own existence, perhaps we shall also determine our destiny. Looking back, we may find the way ahead.

Thus we begin with the discovery that long ago, some 4000 years before Christ, a man walked with his Maker in the cool of a lavish garden. There Adam and his beautiful partner had an existence without death, or most other anxious things that complicate and mar our present life. Nothing but the sky, the beauty, and the joy of sharing life together confronted these two original people. What rules are needed in innocence? What protection in paradise?

Even with all this, the Maker did give them one instruction. They could live unfettered, feasting on all the luscious fruits they could pick, delicious juices running down unblemished chins; life in a never ending state of total bliss, but there was one rule. For some reason they could not partake of the tree in the center of the garden, the tree of the Knowledge of Good and Evil. God had forbidden them this one thing.

So while there was no fear in Eden, no want, no trouble; all was not completely unbridled and fanciful, either. And unknown to the first couple, they had an enemy slithering about in their chamber; God's old antagonist Satan was in the garden, whispering sedition near that curiously forbidden tree.

One immediately wonders why that should have been. What motive did the Creator have in placing this one restriction on the freedom of the first couple? And why give access to the devil at all, and especially in the proximity of a forbidden tree? Why should danger lurk in the form of the old serpent, the enemy of all good, in Paradise at all? Whenever they drew near, as they inevitably did, the serpent would call to the man and his woman. Cunning in ways of seduction he finally managed to co-opt the woman, and against the prohibition of the Maker, she partook of the tree, and her eyes were opened. Here the Bible is unequivocal; this was the greatest disaster that has ever overtaken the race of men.

Afterward things progressed as one might expect. She offered some of the forbidden fruit to the man, and we are told he made a conscious decision to partake of it. While the woman had been deceived, it is asserted that the man decided to go into rebellion to defy the deity, and thus he followed his mate into sin. Whether his motive was to join in sedition, or to simply join his lovely mate in her need, is not well understood, but the Bible tells us she was deceived and he partook with full understanding. Thus the real departure from God was credited to Adam.

Nevertheless both male and female had fallen under the curse; the shroud of mystery we call death. And there was an immediate response. Their light became darkness, and how great the darkness was. Their brilliance vanished, and suddenly they knew they were naked and exposed, full of every anxiety and afraid even of their closest friend, the Maker himself. They would never walk near to him again. They would never walk at ease anywhere, nor would the race of men that came forth from them.

I am sure that in hindsight they may have wondered what could have been wrong with partaking of a fruit whose very name spoke of morality, assuming morality might have some power to make people righteous. Many others who came after them certainly have made a lot of that. After all, it was the fruit of a tree which opened blind eyes to good and evil. Wasn't that what the Maker was all about, good over evil? During his life as a human being, while he walked the earth with mankind, didn't Jesus even ask if "having eyes why could they not see?" It was as if Jesus was asking us if we didn't get it. From the tree men were given eyes to see evil in all its' ugly display.

The serpent had told them the fruit would make them wise, and they were certainly wiser than before. On the other hand they found the knowing of evil was easy, but the doing of good was very hard; and so it has remained until this moment. We desire the good and do evil. But once their eyes had been opened, and they had become accountable for their actions, now they would die.

Innocence fled, followed slowly by the bland dullness that life became, aging their bodies and weakening their minds. To their horror, all other things began to whither as death percolated into everything erupting in continual war in nature. Weeds intruded into beauty, thorns and venom, and warfare and sickness, and finally death. All sorts of rottenness and defilements began to encroach on everything. Science would tell us the Second Law had intervened so that all life was now running down hill, wearing out, and dying. To this day innocence is still being lost, as every day a new child is born into what this world had become.

> For the anxious longing of the creation waits eagerly for the revealing of the sons of God ... For we know that the whole creation groans and suffers the pains of childbirth together until now ... also we groan within ourselves, waiting eagerly for our adoption as sons. (Rom 8:23–25, NASB)

The man now found trouble came to him from inside and out. And a battle has been raging around every son and daughter of mankind ever since. He searches high and low for happiness, he rails against an inner emptiness, and he seeks peace where there is no peace. As a new thing called "time" passed, more and more violations accumulated against the Maker until God repented of having ever made Adam in the first place.

The Flood would wipe most of humankind off the face of the earth; but even after the waves went back into their basins, sin became not only a way of life, it became the very essence of life itself. It is not that man is born to sin but rather he is a sinner inside and out. All he can do is sin. His heart became blackened and there seemed to be no end to the darkness into which men were now plunging.

A great line now passed through the earth. On which side of that great invisible line each one ended up became the most important question confronting every human soul. It is still the great question hovering over every last one of us; from the moment of conception to the end of life. Do we look forward to enjoying the Maker in the glories of everlasting joy, or do we tumble forever into the everlasting blast from below? Every soul of man is eternal; the question is where that soul shall end up. And according to the great Book it is left to each person to make so grave a choice; and a dangerous choice it is. Already the gospel begins to differ from the gnostic message of Calvinism.

9

After the fall men and women were born on the earth and others died. It was relentless. The names of giant intellects passed through the earth like ships in the night. Confucius and Aristotle, Hammurabi and Shakespeare, Kierkegaard and Plato, Bacon, Edison, and even a few moralists like Moses and Socrates, come to mind. But earth's best efforts at making a new beginning were all doomed from the start. All of them had good intentions, most even understood the problem, but until Jesus died on the cross not one of them knew of a way to remove the sin that had come from disobedience in the Garden. They all possessed only the wisdom of the Tree, meaning that they knew what was wrong, but not one thing about making the wrong right again. A few had amazing insights, but in the end every one of them failed to uncover true meaning or even how to escape from this life trapped by a dead end called mortality. Whether the knowledge of Good and Evil comes from within or codified from without, as it does in the Law of Moses, it is not able to produce righteousness. All these thinkers filled our lives with words that wearied the body, swelled the head, and did little for the heart of man. The knowledge of Good and Evil, fruit of the cursed tree, has never led to righteousness, though it has been tried often enough. Meanwhile the really important questions were often abandoned in the hopeless winds of time.

> The words of wise men are like goads, . . . my son, be warned: the writing of many books is endless, and excessive devotion to books is wearying to the body. (Eccl 12:11, 12, NASB)

Chapter 2

John Calvin's Core Beliefs

In THE 1500's ALONG came a brilliant young Catholic theologian, Jean Couvin, known in history by his English equivalent, John Calvin, some twenty years after Luther had posted his famous ninety five thesis on Wittenberg Church door. Calvin had studied theology and law in some of the greatest universities of Europe and would live to receive the title Great Reformer. But like all young men starting out in life, he too was in search of meaning. And because he claimed to be a disciple of Jesus Christ one might have hoped he could provide some answers, but his answers proved to be hopeless and rather terrifying.

Nevertheless, while still in his twenties and a priest in the pay of his local diocese, he had already decided the first human pair had been predestined by God to fall into sin. In other words Calvin believed that God had literally caused the fall of mankind. He reasoned that God had to have known what would happen from the moment they began to enjoy their garden, a paradise with both the devil and the forbidden tree inside. He believed that would make the resulting fall inevitable. And since God knew they would fail, Calvin decided that God had actually forced them to fail. The question for young Calvin was the reason. The cause had to be traced back to the deity himself.

FOREKNOWLEDGE VERSUS FOREORDINATION

In Calvin's thinking God wanted a race of beings made of weak flesh who would stumble and fall into sin. And to be candid, we must admit that Calvin was at least partially right in such an assessment. God didn't have to put the restricted tree into the Garden, nor invite his old nemesis along to provide temptation. We might conclude, as most do, that he was merely testing the first couple. But because of his foreknowledge God already knew the outcome. When God tests us he does so to teach us, and what could he have been teaching Adam and Eve who had no sin in the first place? Adam had no sin of his own to learn about.

So while we know exactly how the thing went down the question still nags as to why. What was the point of having the first couple fall? This is a very important question. It led Calvin to the conclusion that the purpose of mankind on earth was to become the "whipping boy" of God's wrath against sin. Calvin concluded that we were placed on earth to demonstrate God's hatred of sin.

In Calvin's judgmental way of thinking, God needed a sinful race upon which to unleash his sovereignty over evil. Apparently Calvin's god could not show his sovereign righteousness by any other means than to punish some new race he called men. Men were going to be evil from birth, spending their lives in nothing but depravity, and by this God would demonstrate his hatred for sin. Only a few human beings called the "elect" would be chosen before birth to demonstrate that he was still a God of mercy.

But in all his lawyerly analysis Calvin fell into an error about God's foreknowledge which followed him throughout the rest of his life. He believed that the very fact God knew the future meant that God concocted the future. This implied to Calvin that every detail of life was already under the direct control of God. Predestination was not only a doctrine of theology; Calvin believed every thought, every act and every nuance of human life was under the predestined control of God. Whether they knew it or not, whether people could sense it or not, mankind was composed of puppets on a string, and could be nothing else. The script for each life was written before birth.

Now some might attribute such ravings to youth. But Calvin stubbornly kept to his initial views of almost everything. Very young when he wrote his great opus *Institutes of the Christian Religion,* it is amazing that although some years later he did an updated edition, in which he made the thing many times longer, he never changed his mind about anything. Most people grow more cautious with age, but not this man. Instead of a mellowed out Calvin, his role as inquisitor of Geneva increased his harsh fanaticism and his desire to control as he aged.

Still, we must remember that Calvin did not come to his conclusions in a vacuum. Calvin had a mentor, or at least you might say he had a hero, who spoke to him from ages past. He read his favorite church father, St. Augustine, slavishly. Augustine, writing from the fourth century of Christian endeavor, seemed to harden him into a Christianized brand of predestination verging on the fatalism of Augustine's own father's gnostic cult. He came to believe that human beings were doubly predestined into two camps; many for judgment, and a select few for salvation. Not knowing how the deity chose those he chose for election, he assumed they were saved at random without reference to any moral criteria whatsoever. Calvin regarded Augustine to be the height of spiritual piety, and today's Calvinists still regard Augustine with almost Apostolic stature. Listen to John Walvoord, former head of Dallas Seminary:

> . . . [Augustine] crystallized the theology which preceded him, [and] . . . laid the foundations for both Catholic and Protestant doctrine . . . [some] refer to Augustine as "incomparably the greatest man who was 'between Paul the Apostle and Luther the Reformer . . . [1]

Calvin, though still a priest in training, had also been reading the books of the Reformer Luther, and soon regarded himself as part of the Reformation; protesting the excesses and confusion of the Roman Church. So it is somewhat strange that Calvin chose

1. Walvoord, John F., *Bibliotheca Sacra* 108, 416

Augustine the dogmatic proponent and protector of Catholicism, to become his main source of inspiration. But Calvin writing his *Institutes* some 1100 years after St. Augustine, brought into them much of this early church leader's thinking, and attributed nearly everything he wrote to the one he called "that holy man."

We will hear much more about this early churchman Augustine later, but in the meanwhile we view with some measure of amazement how much pull this Catholic statesman had on John Calvin. Even to this present hour, despite his defense of even the most noxious anti-biblical dogmas still resident in much of Catholic doctrine, Augustine remains an icon among Calvinists. Actually this makes us a little suspicious that Calvinism is not so far from Catholic doctrine as they loudly proclaim. Somehow Augustine has become known to supposedly protestant Calvinists as the Protestant's Protestant, while remaining the Catholic's Catholic to the "Holy See." And can we truthfully say he has managed to cause much confusion in both?

Making the mistake of following his ancient mentor more closely than the Word of God, Calvin fell under Augustine's shadow and adopted the trappings of gnostic fatalism which seemed to lap over into Augustine's Christianity. Such a theory of Augustine's theology is often denied by Augustine's biographers. They think they know him well enough to know that he moved cleanly away from his father's gnosis, and so they deny that he retained even a propensity toward being a fatalist. But is it not likely that after spending a near decade of belonging to Manichaeism that Augustine might not ever be completely rid of all their teaching? And from what we do have of his writings, Augustine in his later debates seemed prone toward developing a gradually increasing fatalism that had seeped into his Christianity. Gnostics during the fourth century all claimed to have a deeper *gnosis* or knowledge about spiritual truth than mere Christians, and his father's Manichaeism was one of those cults most dedicated to fatalist ideas. Fatalism, regardless of its' flavor, locks every human being into some kind of lifelong predestination. Gnostics believed that men were destined by the position of the stars, but perhaps in the case of Calvinism, the electing power of God. Calvin may also have borrowed something from his fellow Reformer, Luther whose *Bondage of the Will* is still the classic in the genre of predestination so prevalent for that time. But wherever he got it, Calvin decided that God predestined man for sin. And this was not just a situation in which man was prone to fall by accident; man fell into sin by God's design, or into what Calvinists still call "Total Depravity." And Bible Christian beware, Total Depravity is not just a fancy word for the fallen nature of man.

A person in Total Depravity is not even able to read the Word of God nor listen to and understand the gospel in any form whatsoever. Total Depravity is quite literally the condition of being unable to be saved. Calvin simply asserts that God was condemning most of the human race to hell. It is not well known that embedded in his *Institutes of the Christian Religion,* Calvin actually taught this very thing. Adam fell into sin so that in executing judgment God might be glorified. Listen to the chilling words which come from the pen of Calvin himself:

> God not only foresaw the fall of the first man, and in him the ruin of his posterity; but also at his own pleasure arranged it . . . The decree, I admit, is dreadful; and yet it is impossible to deny that God foreknew what the end of man was to be before he made him, and foreknew, because he had so ordained by his decree.[2]

Here in bold print Calvin actually declares that God made Man for everlasting destruction. Why God should have desired such a thing after walking in loving fellowship with Adam in the Garden is never explained. But God's love for mankind seemed to have gotten lost in the darkness of Total Depravity, and was now limited to the sun and the rain which falls on both the elect and those who are not.

Over and over again we discover that love was not one of Calvin's favorite subjects. Being greatly offended with the sins of others, he yearned for the thunder, for the heavy hand of God in

---

2. Calvin, John, *The Institutes of the Christian Religion,* Book III, 8

vengeful destruction. He never spoke very much at all about the still small voice of love for the sinner, or anyone else. Even the word "love" appears less than one hundred times in his multi thousand page three volume theology, *The Institutes of the Christian Religion*.

Not to make this into some modern victim mentality thing, it is quite apparent that Calvin had never experienced much love. During his long and often dyspeptic life, love was hardly ever on the docket. Forced for appearance sake by nearly everyone he knew into a marriage with a young widow, Idellette de Bure, in his diaries he reveals he was none too happy about it. He even called her a heretic because she was an Anabaptist (she accepted believer's baptism) something Calvin would later pursue to the stake. Still childless from her marriage to Calvin, she died nine years later, though her loss never seemed to bother Calvin very much.

Even his relationship with the Almighty seemed to have been more adversarial than happy. Not trusting in God's love, and terribly afraid of the deity in the sky just waiting to crush him, he spent many days in sickness and angst. And while the fear of God may have been the beginning of wisdom for many, it certainly didn't do much for Calvin. It is more than likely such neurotic fear led Calvin to many misconceptions about the God he is supposed to have been serving for many years.

One major wrong turn was the built in moral dilemma found in Calvinism's predestination which followers of Calvin still face to the present. Most advocates of Calvin have not thought through all the implications but that does not diminish the problem. Predestination as the Reformers defined it implies that every nuance of life is controlled by invisible strings. Man becomes some sort of puppet and all of life has been scripted ahead of us. Calvinists believe that every thought, every act and every event are the result of the sovereign control of God. Nothing ever actually originates inside the mind of the person doing it because the sovereign God put it there. This means that whatever you do it is God pulling the strings to make you do it. All of life is scripted so that Calvin was just being honest when he admitted that in his world God caused Adam and Eve to sin. But even in Calvin's world, to cause another to sin so that you might punish him for doing it, makes a mockery out of any theory of justice known, especially the justice of a perfect God. That would be like the kid caught with his hand in the cookie jar accusing his mother for placing the cookies inside the jar. According to Calvin God had to punish mankind for sin he caused mankind to commit, and that is not really Cricket even to staunch Calvinists.

It has to be an embarrassment to the more savvy people who follow Calvin; the pastors and scholars. Most run of the mill Calvinists probably don't know the problem exists, but those who do must become uneasy, And there is no doubt it is true because many Calvinists try to dodge and minimize this bit of Calvinist minutia by dredging up their usual safety valve, the secret decision making process enclosed within the Godhead itself. God choosing to punish Adam for sin that he himself caused is so repugnant to logic and fairness that it has to be hidden. So like anything Calvinists cannot explain they file it into the Godhead using the Calvinist aphorism. It was all just "according to the pleasure of the secret will of God." If such a thing was decided by God in his own counsels, it is outside the range of human participation. In other words it is no longer something of human concern. This is the way Calvinists always dismiss something they find a bit problematic. Locked inside the Godhead there is no more need of a human explanation, ever.

Calvin had quite a number of such things that were hidden in the pleasure of God's secret counsel. These are the talks which supposedly take place among the members of the Trinity. (Of course we wonder how Calvin got access to know what goes on in such an inner sanctum.) But over the years Calvin and Calvinists seem to have been able to blame a great deal on God's own secret internal consultation.

Meanwhile modern Calvinists blather on that Calvin was always right, and that God caused everything to happen for the general good of all men. But if Calvin was right, and God was utterly just and correct in demonstrating his own sovereign will by taking out his wrath against sin by the destruction of fallen man, then more than four fifths of the human race are already condemned to an eternity in the Lake of Fire, and it was all his fault. And while Jesus did tell us that the broad road leads to destruction, he wanted us to avoid that road, and take the narrow way. But Calvin's theology put a huge road block in front of the narrow way, and made this latter road impassible by human will. So Calvin's way does not sound like such a good idea to me. Perhaps Jesus was lying to us when he warned us about choosing the wrong road. According to Calvin, it is not even possible to choose.

> "If your right eye makes you stumble, tear it out and throw it from you; for it is better for you to lose one of the parts of your body, than for your whole body to be thrown into hell. If your right hand makes you stumble, cut it off and throw it from you; for it is better for you to lose one of the parts of your body, than for your whole body to go to hell. (Matt 5:29–30, NASB)

But instead of looking at what the Scriptures say about heaven and hell, Calvin was following the logic of a system he had fashioned in his mind, much of it from reading Augustine. Because of the logic train we shall be showing soon, it all made perfect sense to him. With his lawyerly mind Calvin believed he had happened onto the real purpose for human existence. Man existed for nothing more than to become the "punching bag" for the righteous indignation of an offended God. And no matter how crude that sounds it is the truth as stated from a Calvinist perspective. God would elevate himself by torturing sinful mankind forever. He would allow only a few, his specially picked out "elect," to escape from such everlasting punishment. Perhaps the few that escape would demonstrate mercy in the midst of judgment, but we don't know how they are chosen because once again, they are tapped out, "according to the pleasure of his secret counsel." The truth of how they are chosen is hidden away inside the Godhead with so many other things Calvin does not want to talk about.

Calvin's detractors often ask a simple question that Calvin could never answer because it is all supposedly hidden away inside of the Trinity. "If God decided to arbitrarily save some, why couldn't he do it for all?" Is God capricious deciding who shall live and who shall die without consideration of any of the factors inside the Bible? Of course there is no answer to this question except to postulate a god who made such a decision "according to the pleasure of his secret will," and for some reason he did not want that dreaded "Universalism," the saving of all men everywhere. Calvinists hate being called universalists almost as much as being called Arminians. But Christ tells us that because of his love for all men and women he wants to be a universalist, but man refuses to cooperate:

> The Lord is not slow about His promise, as some count slowness, but is patient toward you, not wishing for any to perish but for all to come to repentance. (1 Pet 3:9, NASB)

Calvinists blatantly try to placate others with their non-explanation of the workings of the Godhead. Certainly the god of Calvinism is far less loving and forgiving than we have been led to believe through the stories of Jesus in the New Testament. The god of Calvinism seems to have only a little love for this creature of flesh and blood he created. The god of Calvinism seems to be quite different than the God of the Bible as pictured below:

> When I consider Thy heavens, the work of Thy fingers, The moon and the stars, which Thou has ordained; What is man, that Thou dost take thought of him? And the son of man, that Thou dost care for him? Yet Thou hast made him a little lower than God, And dost crown him with glory and majesty! Thou dost make him to rule over the works of Thy hands. (Ps 8:3–6, NASB)

Calvin used classical logic in his theology and finally got off the track because of it. One might have hoped he would have amended his theology and corrected his trajectory sometime during his long life. One enormous mistake was his decision to make no distinction between what God knows about the future, and how he causes it to happen. But once Calvin got over the mental hurdle of God as the causative agent for sin, his religion became unrepentantly deterministic. Both the elect and the non-elect had a script written for their lives, and there was no getting rid of it. God was now the author of sin regardless of the clear teaching found in the Book of James which says that God cannot sin nor can he tempt men to sin.

> Let no one say when he is tempted, "I am being tempted by God"; for God cannot be tempted by evil, and He Himself does not tempt anyone. (Jas 1:13, NASB)

But through Augustine Calvin was locked into predestination. And once there it seemed a callous indifference about "non-elected" people began to seep into him and the millions of others who have followed him. It is still the case today. Calvinists are not very worried about helping and loving. It is rare to find a Calvinist ministry feeding the poor, helping the sick, or evangelizing the world, though they would demur, and it is to be expected that present day Calvinists like John Piper, who seems wildly in favor of overseas missions, would claim otherwise. But when the first American missionary, Adoniram Judson, felt God was calling him to Burma in the late 1800's, he was told by his Calvinist pastor, "if God wants to save the heathen, he is quite capable of making that happen without the likes of you." Fortunately for the heathen, and the modern missionary movement, Judson decided to listen to God.

If man is in the world only to receive judgment, why care about what God doesn't care very much about, anyway? It is quite evident in his own story arc. Soon it would not be difficult for Calvin to condemn many people to burn at the stake. If they were only the "riff raff" God didn't care much about anyway, why not just give them a push in the direction of judgment? In Geneva hideous public executions eventually became common.

LACK OF ASSURANCE

The elect, according to typical Calvinist explanation, were all tapped out in an arbitrary way by God before the world came to be, and the un-elect also, in double predestination. Those not elected are allowed a few years to grow up and work under the sun, but in short order all eventually succumb to death and fall into the furnace.

But this is where the real problems for Calvinists begin. Arbitrary tapping out has caused huge confusion because nobody in Calvinism knows how to perfectly discern their own election. Nobody can remember ever encountering God before he or she was born so not one person is certain he or she is one of those "elected" people. Even Calvin had never been told in eternity past if he was really saved or not, and even if a Calvinist believed he was one of the "elected few" he could not prove it, not even to himself. There is no Scripture which can backup such a claim. There is no Scripture that tells the Calvinist that he was "regenerated" before he was born, but that is exactly what Calvinism is saying. Calvinism makes the incredible claim that people are regenerated (saved) prior to being born! Calvinists try to cobble together various scripture references, but when checked out in context every reference they use falls apart. (We will be looking at "boiler plate" Calvinist verses very soon.)

So this has left Calvinists with the strange prospect of using works to prove they are even saved. These are the people that complain about Biblical Christians using the terminology of "accepting Christ," which Calvinists are sure is a work, and yet Calvinists are stuck using many works to try in vain to prove their own election. They must prove they are the best people alive, which is quite an undertaking. So they start to perform. Reading their Bibles and helping little old ladies cross the street, anything to make themselves look more Christian. And eventually all Calvinists must succumb to this "proof trap of legalism" as the only means of proving themselves to other Calvinists, and even to the harshest critic of all, themselves. If they slack off for even a moment or fall back into even the smallest sin, as they must by just being alive, every single Calvinist gets an overwhelming feeling that they might not be going to heaven at all. Even those at the head of large ministries and churches, names of famous Calvinists, would surprise us with their doubts. Some have even voiced their despair.

RC Sproul is the man they used to call Mr. Calvinist. He was once a leading professor of Calvinism at almost every Reform seminary in America. He is not just a Calvinist, but a world class teacher of Calvinism. But RC Sproul, with all his degrees and accolades never had any peace about his own salvation. Listen as he tells this from his own perspective:

> A while back I had one of those moments . . . [and] the question hit me: 'RC what if you are not one of the redeemed? What if your destiny is not heaven?' . . . I went to my room . . . [and] on my knees I said, 'I can't point to my obedience. There's nothing I can offer . . . I know that some people [the Bible Christians] flee to the cross to escape hell . . . '[but instead he decided it was better to be, in his own word "uncomfortable" with Jesus, than to have an assurance of salvation from the cross.][3]

Here was one of the leading Calvinists on earth and still he had to sadly admit that as a Calvinist he could not flee to the cross as others often do. But according to the Bible that is exactly what the sinner must do. In that instant of insight Sproul ought to have understood how foolish his hope in some esoteric tapping out really was. But he is gone now, and we sincerely hope he had saving faith before he left. But here is the leading Calvinist on earth at his death, and he had no assurance he was even saved. We would be surprised at what other stars of Calvinism doubt their own election.

Soon we will be looking in detail at the logic chain Calvin followed to get to where he was, but Calvinists have a link in that chain known as the TULIP they call "Perseverance." They believe they will persevere to the end of their lives and so be saved in the end. But according to Sproul it is based on a constant state of "being uncomfortable with Christ" a slightly encrypted way of saying that they have no Scripture to back up their beliefs. In truth of fact their "perseverance" is based only on bravado and emotion and not solidly on the Word of God. How can you have assurance if

---

3. Sproul, RC, *Tabletalk*, 20.

you are bearing up under your own effort? The Bible is the only source of stability known to the practice of Christianity.

People sin a whole lot more than they know (what is not of faith is sin), and every sin produces nagging doubt, even for the Bible Christian, until he finds an answer in the Bible. What can the Calvinist do? If leading Calvinists like Sproul cannot find any security in their faith, what can the ordinary Calvinist turn to? Sproul says he cannot cling to the cross. So instead of the all sufficient sacrifice made by the Lamb of God, Calvinists cling to some imagined tapping out in eternity past. It is actually quite amazing.

The terrible fate of these leading Calvinists ought to be a lesson in the use of the Word of God. As the verse below explains, there is no faith without hearing the Word of God. And when you read the Word you don't fly off into wrong thinking and wrong teaching.

> So faith comes from hearing, and hearing by the word of Christ. (Rom 10:17, NASB)

But since they have so little Scripture they can't prove they are saved, let alone tapped out by God for something they call the "elect." Calvinists end up being exactly like Catholics, liberal protestants, and cultists, all who have abandoned the safety of God's Word and long for assurance that they are saved. But there is no assurance outside the never changing foundation of God's Bible truth. They long for assurance, but there is no assurance in Calvinism. Calvinists can never relax until they open their Bibles and come to trust in the Savior, the only way they can come to him. Sproul was correct, all believers must "run to the cross" where Christ paid for their salvation.

> . . . for the same Lord is Lord of all, abounding in riches for all who call on Him; for "Whoever will call on the name of the Lord will be saved." (Rom 10:12-13, NASB)

Trusting transient emotions rather than the unchanging Word always leads to a snare. In Galatians Paul warns against trying to work ones way to heaven. He even calls out to those who think that by starting with truth they will be made perfect with law keeping; he says they are bewitched. But it is so deep within our humanity that we must earn our way. We don't like to simply rest in Christ, so we start well and often end up trying to improve ourselves with works.

But if someone starts out with error, such as Calvin promulgated, and then try to make themselves acceptable by trying to appease God with good works, it must be so much worse. Such people never know where to go for forgiveness. So long as you work, trying to make yourself right before God, the objective you seek will keep moving away, like a mirage in the desert.

Using a water metaphor, you start by trusting in the life jacket called Christ to hold you up from sinking to the bottom. But it is like you have a piano on your back, so you can no longer depend on the jacket. So you begin treading water. But try as you might you can't keep from sinking so long as you are working for salvation.

Drop the piano and the jacket will bear you up. Trust in his Word and with Peter you may walk on the water. Without trust you feel you are drowning, slipping under, never to rise again, that piano taking you straight down. It is not only impossible to make yourself acceptable before a holy God, but the moment you lose trust in the unchanging Word, that which holds you up like the life jacket, is the moment you fall out of grace. You take your hands off the life preserver and grab hold of the piano, and you start to flounder. If you have been saved, you don't stop being saved, but you lose all sense that God is in your life.

THE LOVE OF CHRIST

Along with misunderstanding the difference between foreknowledge and fore-ordination, and the lack of assurance that comes from trusting in the Word of God, the love of God is very scarce in Calvin's *Institutes*.

> We have come to know and have believed the love which God has for us. God is love, and the one who abides in love abides in God, and God abides in him. (1 John 4:16, NASB)

As we have stated, Calvin actually believed that God made the race of human beings to act as eternal "whipping boys" to illustrate his own holiness and his utter separation from sin. The whipping boy was a slave in the antebellum South who would take beatings that spoiled slave owner children were supposed to be getting. But John's emphasis on the love of Christ shows that Calvin's conclusion must be error. God did not make mankind for anything like a "whipping boy."

Calvin never seemed to understand the love of God. If Calvinists need to hear one message it is that God has never been in the terrible process of sending the entire human race to hell in order to demonstrate his sovereignty. That was one of Calvin's main errors. Calvinists have put God on the wrong side. It is the devil which hates mankind. Rather than destroying mankind, God has been saving in order to demonstrate his sovereignty.

And for those who misunderstand the intensity of the love relationship between God and man as demonstrated by his cross, Jesus has provided a parable which leading Calvinists love to misinterpret to their own detriment, because ironically they think it makes their point. The section of Scripture in Luke opens with a lawyer expounding the Law of Moses, how people ought to respond to God. But remember the Law is perfect and no man except the Son can obey the Law.

> And a lawyer stood up and put Him [Jesus] to the test, saying "Teacher, what shall I do to inherit eternal life?' And [Jesus] said to him "What is written in the Law? How does it read to you?" And he answered , "You shall love the Lord your God with all your heart, and with all your soul, and with all your strength, and with all your mind; and your neighbor as your self." (Luke 10:25–27, NASB)

The Calvinist who is preaching this parable immediately takes the side of the lawyer and the Law of Moses. You must love God with all your heart, and with all your soul, and with all your strength, and with all your mind in order to be saved? And who can do any of that? We don't even know how to do that. How does one love with all their hearts and souls and minds? In effect we are lost before we begin, and for both sides that is just the point they are in pursuit of.

For the Calvinist. the point is made that in this world nobody can be saved except those tapped out and regenerated (given new life) supernaturally before they are born. Their point is that for Calvinists the saved do not come from this world, they come from another somewhere before they are born, where God gives them eternal life.

The Calvinist will add that the parable following, where Jesus tells about the Samaritan is an illustration of the same thing. Calvinists believe that it is added to illustrate what an impossible love looks like. So that the two religious authorities, the Levite and the priest, are about as good as can be expected, as they pass by feeling sorry on the other side of the road. The Calvinist tells us that such love as that provided by the Samaritan is too high and holy for any of us in this world. We are all like the Levite and the priest, and God is trying to show us as we are, impossible to save by making a personal decision in this world.

But the parable actually comes about because the lawyer has asked Jesus who his neighbor is, referring to the tiny post script at the end of the legal verse about how to love God through the Law. Here in the tiny post script is where Jesus begins his parable, it is well known to all:

> "A man was going down from Jerusalem to Jericho, and fell among robbers, and they stripped him and beat him, and went away leaving him half dead. And by chance a priest was going down on that road, and when he saw him, he passed by on the other side. Likewise a Levite also, when he came to the place and saw him, passed by on the other side. But a Samaritan, who was on a journey, came upon him; and when he saw him, he felt compassion, and came to him and bandaged up his wounds, pouring oil and wine on them; and he put him on his own beast, and brought him to an inn and took care of him." (Luke 10:30–34, NASB)

Jesus never disagrees with the thesis that the Law is too hard for human beings to obey. Nobody will ever go to heaven by attempting obedience to the Law, which is part of the point he is also making, and here he agrees with Calvinists and the lawyer. But in that small addition on the end, the part about the neighbor, is where Jesus describes a better "Royal Law" which does save us.

And what is here? A man, a hated resident of the old northern kingdom, which years before had been invaded and inundated with Assyrians so the population was assimilated and mixed. Such were the Samaritans, rejected members of a mongrel people, a despised and rejected race. Nobody in Israel would expect such a person to do anything except join the robber gangs that often waylaid people on the steep and winding road between Jerusalem and Jericho.

But this Samaritan, a man well acquainted with sorrows, a half breed (part Jew and part Gentile) reminds us of another despised and rejected "half breed"! We call him Jesus, himself the man of sorrows, who will soon be wounded for the sins of men. He is fully God and fully man, a sort of "half breed" from heaven. (And it may be of interest that most Jews mistakenly believed that Jesus really was a half breed. The virgin birth had led to many tales that Jesus was the child of an illicit affair between Mary and a Roman guard.)

The Samaritan is a man who is considered unclean, but he touches the unclean wounds of the man on the road and makes them clean. In an interesting comparison, the Holy Spirit is making here, a comparison I believe he wants us to see, Jesus is the man who is spiritually clean, but who will touch the filthy wounds of the unclean (really all mankind lying beside the road to destruction) and whose touch makes them clean. And in the process he will take on their sin to become unclean himself like the serpent on the pole in Numbers. He will take on the sin of the world. The Samaritan is the man who is ritually unclean who by his love is touching the filthy wounds of a man he does not even know and by doing so becoming spiritually clean. And by the way Jesus wants our lives to look this way too. This is the Royal Way, the Royal Law.

The good Samaritan binds up the wounds of this man with the oil and wine as Jesus will wash the wounds of our sin and anoint us with the oil of the Holy Spirit. As the Samaritan loads the wounded man onto his own beast and carries him away to safety, so also Jesus will carry our wounded spirits away from the danger of hell to a place of safety.

Jesus the perfect clean Lamb picks us all up on the road to destruction, touches our filthy wounds of sin and cleans them, and like the brazen serpent on Moses pole becomes unclean. The unclean Samaritan cleans the wounds of the broken man and binds them becoming the true lover of the man. Finally at the inn the Samaritan promises to take care of the man's needs and will return to make sure all is well with him. After our wounds of sin are bound the Son of Man goes away but promises he will return to ensure our eventual home in heaven, far from the demonic gangs along the road.

Both the lawyer and Jesus agree that no man obeys the Law of Moses. But Jesus brings a solution to this young lawyer and to us. A new law, the "Royal Law." When men love their neighbors they are also loving God, and in loving God by loving others they have fulfilled the Royal Law that leads to heaven.

God in Jesus loves mankind. He will get down into the blood and the gore and bear away our wounds of sin. More than that, someday he will return to take home those whom he has covered up with the wine and the oil. Jesus is the good Samaritan. More than that he demonstrated in this parable how to love God through loving our neighbor, even the neighbor we didn't even know we had. The Calvinist is wrong and profoundly wrong. We must obey the Royal Law, and become more like the Samaritan, and less like the priest and the Levite who would not get involved. Calvinists believe that the lost cannot be helped. Once again they violate the direct command of Jesus. Listen to Calvinist Spurgeon:

> As it is my wish [and] your wish . . . so it is God's wish that all men should be saved . . . he is no less benevolent than we are.[4]

4. Hunt quoting Spurgeon. Hunt, *What Love Is This?*, 47.

> My little children, I am writing these things to you ... He
> Himself is the propitiation [payment] for our sins; and
> not for ours only, but also for those of the whole world.
> (1 John 2:1–2, NASB)

Scripture states clearly that Jesus was the payment for the sins of the whole world; not just some few called the "elect" who are born already "regenerated." In the face of this verse the whole debate is really over. Jesus paid for the sins, was the propitiation for every single one of us long before we were born. Everything Calvin affirms is contradicted in these few words. Christ even promises to be our Advocate. But why should we need a defense attorney, an Advocate, when according to Calvinism the verdict is already in the hand of the judge and it is guilty?

THE CROSS

Calvin's answer to the greatest question asked by mankind is horrendous. Since in his mind God actually caused the fall, and it is axiomatic that man was created to be judged, then most men are locked into Total Depravity, which is a sentence to hell. In Total Depravity man is unable to confess his sins and receive the Holy Spirit. All those born into this world without having been regenerated before time would end up in awful Total Depravity, and finally the Lake of Fire.

So while they may sing the song, no Calvinist actually "clings to the old rugged cross," because they think it is futile. Even though Calvin admitted that a few un-elected people might for a time cling to the Savior by their own decision, they would soon tire of the demands of salvation and fall away again.

But let us examine the cross further; what it means to Calvinists and what it means to Christians. On the night of his anguish, blood dripping from his face, Jesus' prayer tells us what is coming.

> 'Father save me from this hour'? But for this purpose I
> came ... Father, glorify Your name." Then a voice came
> out of heaven: "I have both glorified it, and will glorify it

again." And I, if I am lifted up from the earth, will draw all men to Myself." (John 12:27,31, NASB)

The Bible clearly states that the cross is God's remedy for the lostness of man, and it mentions no other. Christ's death is the only antidote to the fall in the garden. But in their heavy focus on judgment and sovereignty Calvinists forget that God told the whole world his first attribute would always be love, and his mercy is everlasting. In fact God tells us that it is his very nature to love:

> everyone who loves . . . knows God. The one who does not love does not know God, for God is love . . . By this the love of God was manifested in us, that God has sent His only begotten Son into the world so that we might live through Him.(1 John 4:7–9 NASB)

His mercy pleads with every human being to turn from his sin, accept his forgiveness and live, something patently impossible if Calvin is right. A person who is in Total Depravity cannot even hear such a plea.

> For God did not send the Son into the world to judge the world, but that the world might be saved through Him. (John 3:17, NASB)

But if Calvin is correct, and man is on this planet only to showcase God's wrath, then why bother with the cross in the first place? It becomes nonsense. Why do you launch a rescue to save people that can't be rescued? And if the cross is nonsense, why birth the Son of God into a man's body in order to die in agony in place of those who can't be saved? If most people arrive in this life un-elected and without even the possibility of being saved, the cross and all the offers of Christ must be seen as a mockery. Why bother to rescue a creature you know you are about to destroy? We actually wonder if Calvinists really have any use for the cross at all.

Famous preacher John Piper proclaims himself to be a "seven point Calvinist," whatever that means. In 1997 his church published a document to clarify their church position on the cross of Christ. The primary purpose of the printed memorandum was to inform visitors to their church about their Reformed stand on several issues. One issue was the Reform view of the sacrifice Christ made on the cross, and it helps us to understand how Calvinists look at the heart of the Christian faith. As we stated earlier, we wonder if the cross even matters to Calvinists, and as it turns out, it almost doesn't. To quote from their document:

> We do not deny that all men are the intended beneficiaries of the cross in some sense . . . what we deny is that all men are . . . beneficiaries . . . in the same way . . . every time the gospel is preached to unbelievers it is the mercy of God that gives this opportunity for salvation.[5]

Such a brochure was published as a notice to church visitors. It was designed to assuage and deflect Bible Christians from leaving as fast as they came through the door. (Even Calvinists want numbers in their churches.) It must be understood that Pastor John Piper knows very well that his Reform view of Christ is not the same as what is taught in Bible churches. So using the traditional (Bible) understanding of ordinary believers, it attempts to obscure the differences Calvinists actually teach on the most central doctrine of our faith, the cross of Christ.

The implication as intended is that Christ is giving everyone the same opportunity for salvation, and if this were true the argument is largely over. We would have to say that Calvinists believe the same gospel as Bible Christians. Unfortunately even here they have to confess to the strange idea that the cross does not work the same for all people. So the first part of the brochure communicates the truth that Reform churches actually believe. The cross does not work the same for all people. Piper is telling those who come through his door that the cross is for everyone, but not everyone in the same way. Toward the end of the document the pastoral staff of this Reform body say that the cross gives everyone an "opportunity for salvation." These words are parsed out very carefully and are not entirely forthright in their meaning. Unknown to most visitors "the opportunity" is snatched out from under their feet, because as they put it, "the cross works differently for different people."

---

5. Piper, John, Church position paper, 14.

What visitors won't hear is that only those chosen from before the world was created will ever be told the cross saves them.
And for the others this so-called "opportunity for salvation" actually works to their injury because it leads to yet another rejection
of Christ and more judgment to face. The Totally Depraved, un-
elected person is assumed to always be rejecting the gospel, which
keeps adding to his eventual condemnation.

Reform people often cloak what they actually believe in traditional Bible jargon. The brochure is carefully worded to avoid
lying and yet leave an impression of conservative Christian salvation that is almost a direct contradiction to what John Piper actually believes. Calvinists do not really believe the preaching of the
gospel will save anyone who is in this world. When they preach to
large crowds they are not doing evangelism in the mode of a traditional evangelist like Billy Graham, who is trying to get individuals
to take Jesus as Savior. In their minds they are filtering out those
with Total Depravity, and seeking after the "elect," who they will
attempt to disciple into Calvinism.

So there is no real "opportunity for salvation" open to the
non-elect, as suggested by this brochure in a Calvinist church.
When the gospel is proclaimed in Piper's church, or anywhere else
in the Reformed world, the evangelist is looking for people God
has already tapped out and regenerated. You must already be saved
to respond to the Reformed Gospel, and these are the people Calvinists are seeking after to join their churches.

As for the person who is Totally Depraved, it does not matter how sincerely a confession is made, it is all for naught. On the
other hand no Calvinist ever knows who is and who is not Totally Depraved. So such a person who responds in a group setting
would be readily accepted into a Calvinist body. Calvinists actually
doubt that few if any Totally Depraved persons will ever respond
to an altar call because of a natural distaste for all that is spiritual,
but they would never know if such a person actually had.

Nevertheless, for such a person their destiny is already set,
and Christ is not their advocate. Unless the inquirer is already
part of the elect from before he was born, he is lost. Christ on that

old rugged cross apparently has no power to save anyone who is already in this present world. But remember Christ spoke of those who appear Godly but seem to deny the power thereof. Perhaps he was speaking about Calvinists. They do deny the power of the cross to save anyone.

Paul declared victory in the death and resurrection of Christ to bring salvation to the vilest sinner. Apparently Paul believed in the power of the Gospel message to save sinners in the here and now, and we are convinced that Piper must be taking the words of Calvin over the words of the Apostle Paul, never a very wise thing to do.

> For I am not ashamed of the gospel for it is the power of God for salvation to everyone who believes, to the Jew first and also to the Greek. (Rom 1:16, NASB)

In Calvin's world, except for those responding because they were already regenerated from before they were born, conversions that happen on the spot, during evangelistic crusades and by personal invitation to ask Christ into one's life, are all fake. Calvin himself mocked such conversions as "emotional" and predicted they would fade. In a Calvinist meeting, "when the gospel is preached," it is not an "opportunity" for salvation as the Piper brochure dishonestly intimates, such an "opportunity" being cynically out of reach. Instead it is the net being extended, seeking those who think they were "regenerated" by a sovereign act from time eternal, before they were born. And when such a response is recorded, the Calvinists have to believe it, because there is no way to check it out.

Strangely enough, Calvinists believe faith comes after the new birth, and they tend to think of the entrance of faith as a sort of a moment of enlightenment when the person finally affirms he/she is of the elect. But it is strictly an emotional experience. There is no Scripture to back such an idea up, and it cannot be much different than the "burning in the bosom" a Mormon feels when they come to Mormon "enlightenment."

But all this violates the Scriptures. Late one evening in Jerusalem a Pharisee named Nicodemus came to see Jesus who was there for the Passover feast. Nicodemus was a leading member of the Sanhedrin, the ruling body of the Jews, and the Pharisee sect who were the true conservative Bible scholars of his day. Because he knew the Old Testament, Nicodemus felt a mighty prophet had been raised up for their day, but because of the political atmosphere he came secretly, so as not to be seen by too many inquisitive eyes.

> this man came to Him by night and said to Him, 'Rabbi, we know that You have come from God as a teacher for no one can do these signs that You do unless God is with him. (John 3:2–3, NASB)

But Jesus, looking past the flattery of his words, responded in a peculiar way by referring Nicodemus back to an event in the ancient book of Numbers. It was one of those Old Testament vignettes that even the scholars had never fully understood, and nobody felt it was very important. It is only a tiny interlude in one of the books of Moses.

Poisonous serpents had been biting the people as they journeyed and many were dying from the painful bites. Uncertain to the scholars of Nicodemus' day, it was a picture of sin, and the snakes were like demons injecting spiritual poison. Moses was told to mount a brass serpent on a pole and lift it up so everyone in the camp could see it. And every person who looked at that brazen serpent was instantly healed. Clearly there was no selectivity because every person without exception who simply obeyed and looked was healed.

Jewish scholars knew it was some sort of a teaching about the coming Messiah, but it made no sense to them. Jesus shocked this Bible scholar with the interpretation. He explained to Nicodemus that after his lifting up on the cross he would become the serpent on the pole, which was no different than telling Nicodemus he was Messiah. Then he elaborated, telling Nicodemus something even more life shattering. In the same way that the brass serpent healed all who looked his way, he was going to heal the sin of all those who looked to him, when lifted up on the cross. He was going to heal the wounds of the world. He would take the sin of the world upon himself. Anyone who trusted in his ability to take their sin away would be saved.

These words of Jesus are like a slap in the face to the Calvinist. No special elected group was involved, no tapped out people from before the world was made, just anyone who would come to him, anyone in the whole wide world. Anyone who wanted his sin taken away would find the true antidote, when the true Messiah was lifted up.

> "And I, if I am lifted up from the earth, will draw all men to Myself." (John 10:32, NASB)

Admittedly this story still confuses some Christians because they hate the idea of Jesus being pictured as a poisonous serpent. But his words were a giant revelation. All the people had to do was to look to him in order to live. He would take their sins upon himself and exchange them for his righteousness. God would judge the sin by laying it on Jesus, instead of leaving it on the sinner. The sin that would have killed the sinner was left in the grave.

> Nicodemus said to Him, "How can a man be born when he is old?" . . . [Jesus responded] as Moses lifted up the serpent in the wilderness, even so must the Son of Man be lifted up; that whoever believes in Him should not perish, but have eternal life. (John 3:4, 14, NASB)

Jesus' righteousness would be exchanged for the sinfulness of those "bitten," and dying of sin. And not one thing was mentioned about some tapping out before the world was made. Jesus' words make the cross available to all who want what Jesus has to give. All sin was placed upon him when he declared it was "finished." It was finished from the cross. Jesus had become the brazen serpent, and as John had declared, he was taking the sin of the world away. Nicodemus is told that he must be born again (regenerated), not in some misty past, but by looking to the sacrifice of Christ upon the cross.

> He [the Father] made Him [the Son] who knew no sin to
> be sin on our behalf, so that we might become the righ-
> teousness of God in Him. (2 Cor 5:21, NASB)

Though each and every Jew was part of Israel's Chosen People, nobody in Israel was excluded from this command to look to
Jesus for salvation. Each one had to make a decision to look to the
Savior, and God would do the saving. Being chosen meant nothing
as regards to salvation for Israel. As Jesus explained to Nicodemus,
the brass serpent represented the sacrificial lamb with all the sin of
the world placed upon him. In that moment, when Jesus assumed
all the sin of the earth, even the Father had to look away from his
beloved Son. But only Jesus, the one who had no sin of his own,
could take upon himself the sin of all men. Knowing we are in
Christ, we have the promise of God that we are saved. There is no
tapping out in eternity past, there is no regeneration before we are
born, and there is no faith that comes later to prove we are of the
elect. It was on the cross that Jesus purchased everlasting life for
everyone who wanted it.

> And the witness is this, that God has given us eternal life,
> and this life is in His Son. He who has the Son has the
> life; he who does not have the Son of God does not have
> the life. These things I have written to you who believe in
> the name of the Son of God, in order that you may know
> that you have eternal life. (1 John 5:11–13, NASB)

> There is now no condemnation for those who are in
> Christ Jesus. (Rom 8:1, NASB)

BUT WHY WAS THE TREE IN THE GARDEN?

But the question we puzzled with at the beginning of this little
book still emerges; "Why the tree?" What was God up to when he
put that forbidden tree into Eden's garden? What moved the loving
Father in heaven to put the means of our despair into the paradise
he had made for the first couple? What was God thinking? Why

didn't he just leave Adam and Eve to wander in a state of blissful innocence, forever?

Adam and Eve could have produced a whole world of happy people, innocents who never would have had to pay any attention to moral issues. They would never have known one moment of suffering and pain. There were lots of delicious fruits in the garden to keep them occupied. Nobody needed the fruit on that particular tree.

And what about Calvin and his ugly blaming of God? Was God the author of sin? Surely God did have something to do with the end of that wondrous bliss in Eden. There can be no question that by putting the Tree of the Knowledge of Good and Evil into the garden, God had something to do with what happened during the fall. So are we wrong about Calvin? After all we have seen, are we still wrong? Did God cause the Fall of Man, as Calvin so brazenly wrote? We find ourselves almost afraid to ask. If God was involved in sin, any sin, then Jesus is not the "Lamb without blemish" and only such a "Lamb" can take away the sin of the world. Is it even possible that Calvinists do not understand? Calvin's "answer" makes the cross of no effect. But is there an answer? Yes I think there is. And in answering that question, on the reason God required a race in sin, in the understanding which results we may find answers to the final question, the real purpose for mankind; what we set out to know when we began this quest some forty pages ago.

Human sin began on the day man first disobeyed God, the day Adam took from the forbidden Tree. But why should taking from a tree that gives wisdom on the question of right and wrong bother God? To the natural man it would seem that a knowledge of good and evil might be part of the answer. But such a thing does not prove to be true. Man, in knowing the right, seems unable to do what is right. Even the great Apostle Paul lamented his ability to do what he knew to be right, and the ease with which he could sin shocked him greatly.

> I find then that the principle of evil is present in me, the
> one who wishes to do good. For I joyfully concur with

the law of God in the inner man, but I see a different
law in the members of my body, waging war against the
law of my mind, and making me a prisoner of the law of
sin which is in my members. Wretched man that I am!
Who will set me free from the body of this death? (Rom
7:21–24, NASB)

With Paul we have all followed in our first parent's foot-
steps, and are thus guilty of breaking God's commandments. We
all rightly face death and the judgment coming because we have
sinned. Right from the moment they took of the fruit, the first
couple understood they could no longer stand in the presence
of a holy God. So they ran to hide in the greenery, and covered
themselves with leaves. The leaves are really metaphors for many
excuses, a covering to hide what mankind had become. We still use
the same methods, and even little children know what it means to
try to hide their sin. Sinful people hide in the midst of large cities
hoping that both God and man will never notice them in the midst
of all the rest of that sin.

But it does seem curious that the God who sees all things
and knows all things, stood quietly by and allowed them to take
of what they knew was the forbidden fruit. As we said, it was God
who placed the forbidden tree in the Garden and allowed the Serpent access, so there is no way that he could not have known what
was going to happen. God has the power to see the future, even if
he does not cause it, as Calvin always insisted.

And here is where we finally begin to notice a distinction. In
geometry a slight divergence can result in an infinite change. One
line pulling away from its parallel can quickly lead you light years
away from where you thought you would be. God knew the future,
and he knew about the fall, but that does not mean he caused this
future; foreknowledge is anything but predestination. If Calvin
would have been a better student of Bible, and left off listening to
Augustine, he would have known. Of course God knew what was
going to happen, God knows everything. Not only what will occur
but an infinite number of other possibilities encompassing every
act men might take. God knows not only what will happen but

what could happen if any other of billions of possibilities had intervened. God is never taken by surprise, but according to James, he never sins nor does he tempt anyone else to sin. Still, there is no doubt he knew the forbidden tree would make it easy for the first couple to fail. He had sincerely warned them against the use of the tree, though he knew they would take of it. It was Satan who tempted the first couple. So while we cannot dismiss Calvin's argument that God knew what was coming, we can say with assurance that God did not have any role in making it happen. Unlike Calvin we can and must disassociate God's knowing from God's action.

So when God called out to the errant couple, hiding in the midst of their leaves as though he was trying to find them, it was not because he had lost track of where they were. In all the universe God has never lost track of a single electron. God literally knows everything. He wanted the couple to come out and face him.

When God made the earth; when he planted the Garden of Eden and fashioned the first couple, he knew all this was coming. Revelation even says that Christ was already crucified before the foundation of the world. Calvin did understand a few things. He understood that in the creation of man God was looking for a way to demonstrate something of great importance, because Jesus was set to die on the cross from all eternity. God was looking for a way to demonstrate something far more wonderful than his hatred of sin.

God had been preparing for the rescue of mankind from eternity past. That alone is worthy of some deep meditation. God was preparing for the rescue, and not the destruction of mankind. But we wonder if that can be all that there was to this. It seems there is another ingredient which is often overlooked by most Bible Christians. As poor Tevia in *Fiddler on the Roof* said in the movie, could there have been some vast eternal plan? I think so, and I believe the Bible says so. God actually needed to include the risky business of a fallen race of men in some vast eternal plan. Does God have an even greater plan for mankind than their rescue? To form man out of the ground and then to go to all the trouble to rescue him again seems like a waste of God's time. As awesome and wonderful as the passion of Christ became, was God just spinning his wheels? There must be something more to this story that most Christians are largely missing. What was God doing when he needed a race like Adam to rescue? Calvin thought God was forming a whipping boy to demonstrate his hatred for evil, but was that the end of it? Was that even the beginning?

Perhaps it is starting to dawn on us who explore the greatest questions that man does indeed have some amazing role to play, or why the bother of God in coming to earth to die as the Son of Man in first place? The clues God leaves are like bread crumbs scattered about the Word and lead us to some amazing conclusions. All is so wonderful that I have actually come to believe that the whole of planet earth was created to be a foundation, a place to anchor a cross; the cross of Christ. An enormous foundation for what seems in human eyes a little event, even a side step of history, in the whirling dry dust of the Middle East. Obviously size means nothing to God, and things of enormous consequence have happened there on this minor planet out in the fringe of a medium sized galaxy, one of billions of others. In fact I think we may be approaching the meaning of why humanity was made in the first place, the very thing mankind has been searching for forever.

> To me, [Paul] the very least of all saints, this grace was given, to preach to the Gentiles the unfathomable riches of Christ, and to bring to light what is the administration of the mystery which for ages has been hidden in God who created all things; so that the manifold wisdom of God might now be made known through the church to the rulers and the authorities in the heavenly places. This was in accordance with the eternal purpose which He carried out in Christ Jesus our Lord . . . (Eph 3:8–11, NASB)

Paul is hinting at what God is really up to, if we read between the lines. In fact he may be telling us the reason for mankind's creation in the first place. What caused God to bother with a tiny human entity of flesh and bone, when he already had millions of beings of spirit and majesty? And why did the Creator; the undisputed Lord of all that exists with all its glories, stretching out to infinity, decide to make this tiny earth? This tiny theater for the great drama of redemption over which all creation now groans?

Heaven is outside our universe, perhaps in a higher dimension, or something even so incredible we are not yet even equipped to think about it. But even within the mundane physics of our known universe are objects of such size and power they boggle human imagination. We imagine the Sun to be an object of tremendous power with billions of lumens of light shooting out in all directions. It is an object of such stupendous size you could put a million earths inside our sun, and earth must remain ninety three million miles away or its immense power would render earth a charred cinder in seconds. And yet our sun would vanish from sight next to the largest star we know about. This is Canis Majoris, and you could put a billion of our suns inside this incredible object. Canis seems from the tiny human perspective, to be an object of infinite power. Pluto orbits 3.3 billion miles from earth, and it takes five hours for light from the sun to reach Pluto. But this one star, Canis, if it were placed where the sun is located would engulf the entire solar system and make the orbit of Pluto seem smallish deep in the center of the star! Canis is so immense that human imagination cannot fathom it, and yet our God made it, spoke it into existence with a word. If Canis Majorus is power, truly God is beyond human comprehension. So with such majesties in mind even in our known cosmos, for what incredible purpose did God decide to make man?

> What is man that you think of him, And the son of man
> that You are concerned about him? Yet You have made
> him a little lower than God, And you crown him with
> glory and majesty. (Ps 8:4–5, NASB)

As we have said, the Bible is the only potential source for such information. Perhaps the most ancient portion of this Bible holds a key, and I think it does. Job is the probably the oldest book in the world. So now we open this most ancient book which I think holds the key to why humanity was brought into existence in the first place. Paul has already told us that even angels long to look into such things. I think after we look at the evidence, in the answer may lie a resounding bit of incredible understanding that will resolve Calvin completely.

Chapter 3

The Key is in the Book of Job

IN THIS CHAPTER WE take a slight detour into the very fabric of the Old Testament, and focus on one book, the wonderful old Book of Job. It is what many scholars call the oldest book in the world. Job (pronounced with a long "o") is a very unusual book indeed. Probably written in the years following the Great Flood, this book includes nothing about Israel, since Israel does not yet exist, or anything else that is prominent in the Old Testament. Nor is it intimately connected to the New Testament, with the exception that Job knows his Redeemer is coming and sings his praise.

> Oh that my words were written! Oh that they were inscribed in a book! That with an iron stylus and lead They were engraved in the rock forever! And as for me, I know that my Redeemer lives. And at the last He will take His stand on the earth. Even after my skin is destroyed, Yet from my flesh I shall see God;(Job 19:23–26, NASB)

Still rebounding from the waters of the Flood, the world of Job's time would have been verdant with life everywhere. It would have been especially lush and humid near the equator, like a global greenhouse; in contrast to never ending snows at the poles. High precipitation due to the humidity that resulted from the Flood, would cause great accumulations of snow building up near the poles, pressing down and moving out as continental glaciers. This is the world after the Great Deluge.

Nevertheless without Scripture of any kind, Job seemed to have great insight into the things of God. He looked ahead to a resurrection day when God would save those who love him. Job's song of praise for his Redeemer stands like a foreign language against the stark gloom of Calvinism. Job loved God and knew God loved him in return. Man for loveless Calvin was only a prop upon which the sovereign could execute eternal judgment. For Job the judgment of the Flood was past and he expected to look upward and see the Savior in his resurrected flesh. Job's faith was saving him way before Abraham.

For those who know the book, the main body of this ancient document contains a long debate between Job and his friends who supposedly have come to "help" him understand why his life had suddenly turned so downhill. We who read the Book know but they don't know, why God has seemingly abandoned his servant Job. They debate the meaning of the terrible losses that have come upon his life largely misunderstanding the whole thing. But Job too is blind to the front of the book, where God and Satan have been having a disagreement over the question of love. He has no way to know that his very life has become an experiment.

We are given a ringside seat to watch an interaction between God and his old nemesis the devil, the two most powerful and ancient beings known to humanity. One of them is much greater than the other. God is the Creator of even the devil, but Satan still does wield great power as we shall see. In this short exchange there are many clues about God's deepest purposes; things which are not easily found elsewhere, even in the Bible itself. Along with being a showcase for the enormous difference between these two ancient antagonists, God seems to show what mankind's purpose really is going to be.

We know from the prophets Isaiah and Ezekiel that Satan had once been one of those special angels whose duty is to stand guard around the throne in heaven. But for some unknown reason Satan became proud and sought to become like the "Most High." Isaiah adds a bit of background:

> How you have fallen from heaven, O star of the morning, son of the dawn! . . . But you said in your heart, I will ascend to heaven; I will raise my throne above the stars of God, I will sit on the mount of assembly In the recesses of the north. . . . I will make myself like the Most High. Nevertheless you will be thrust down to Sheol, to the recesses of the pit . . . (Isaiah 14:12–17, NASB)

And we must say that Calvin did have one shrewd insight. While he was wrong about almost everything else, he did seem to understand that man was made for some sort of demonstration. And this does get to the root of the question. There can be no doubt that man was created for a purpose and that purpose is connected to his destiny. And I believe that man's destiny turns out to be far larger than just being himself, larger even than the incredible rescue by Jesus on the cross. In fact God directs angels to look into a very special aspect of the creation and salvation of man, and even reveals to us that someday we shall sit with Jesus as judge of angels.

> As to this salvation, the prophets who prophesied of the grace that would come to you made careful search and inquiry . . . it was revealed that they were not serving themselves, but you, in these things which now have been announced . . . things into which angels long to look.(1 Pet 1:10–12, NASB)

Soon we hope to provide closure that might explain why man was made in the first place, and what this has demonstrated to angels. And I believe this will clarify the whole Calvinist debate by putting it on the right foundation. The church has been struggling with these issues for over 500 years, but perhaps others have been looking in the wrong places. You can never build anything when trying to lay it on the wrong foundation.

But just for argument, if Calvin is right, and mankind is here only to allow God a platform to demonstrate His sovereign indignation against sin, then the human race diminishes to the function of the "whipping boy" on par with the slavery of the antebellum south. And we are left with the imposing vision of a God who is an uncontrollable bully, whose sole purpose is to increase His own majesty by the destruction of our race. But if there is a higher purpose to the creation and fall of man, then Calvin is not only wrong, he has smeared the Almighty God, and led a sizeable portion of the church into a dark heresy.

Since God is the Creator of everything, he is Creator even of the devil who according to the verse we read was once was one of the Cherubim, angels of enormous stature and power who stand by the throne of God. Somehow Satan's mind was twisted and he decided he could raise his throne above the throne of the Almighty Creator God. Lucifer, the bearer of light, became Satan the Accuser, the great enemy of God, and leader of an angelic insurrection against God, all of which may have happened eons in the past before this meeting over Job.

Job seems to have been wealthy and famous in the ancient world. The Bible tells us he and his family lived in a place called the land of Uz, which sounds to our ears like someplace out of a fairy tale and yet modern archeologists say it was real and existed somewhere near southern Israel in what is today the land of Jordan. It is a barren wilderness now, one of the most imposing deserts on planet earth, but then it was rich, well watered, and full of forests and grass. Job had seven sons and three daughters, thousands of cattle, along with numerous sheep, many camels and oxen.

This man of antiquity was happy to serve God with his wealth and his great family. As far as we know Job's family all seemed to fairly glow with the righteous joy of fellowshipping together, and all seem well instructed in ways that please God. His sons invited their brothers and others to share their goods in fellowships and dinners in their homes. Their hospitality was apparently famous, and Job was careful to remind his children to continually follow the Lord in all that they did. So far this all sounds so good.

But then comes the jarring discordance of verse six. God apparently invited in all the angelic host to his throne room to present themselves in some cosmic open house, and Satan came among them also. For some reason this seems to bother a lot of Christians. (How on earth they wonder can Satan have access to the throne room of God?) I guess they expect God to have posted some kind of signs to keep out Beelzebub. But why do they worry? Do they expect God to have any chance of being tainted? God fears no archangel, even if he is the devil. While Satan is an entity of incredible power he comes into the presence of God Almighty. All that can be said is that while Satan is totally evil; capable of "shaking the nations" as the Bible puts it. But God has some sort of purpose in this communication. And we have no reason to doubt that this type of communication goes on even into the present. I actually believe that the whole host of hell was watching this interaction, perhaps on something very akin to close circuit TV, however that works in the spirit world.

God by definition is everywhere; so this business of Satan's coming before him does not really matter as to where it actually took place. At any moment God can speak with anyone across space and time. But wherever it happened, the encounter shows something about the character of these two immense beings. Satan is a bragging sneering show off who seems totally taken up with himself, parading about over the surface of the earth. Does he not understand that the Lord of all that exists knows everything already? But like any common thug he wants to be the center of attention. By contrast God is totally at ease and focused on his servant Job. God never needs to bring glory to himself because God is glory wherever he is.

But in the exchange God points out Job and things begin to happen. Satan makes the case that Job has been protected so that his behavior outwardly appears to be loving God. But Satan wants to make the case that this is nothing but an act. Satan does not believe in selfless love, lives only to serve himself; and Satan believes this is secretly true for every being in existence. Every entity which exists is looking out for number one. And without saying it, Satan even believes this about God. If God weren't so powerful, so powerful that not even the mightiest demon can do anything to him, even he would be shown to be selfish in his motive for love. What bothers Satan is that God is pretending to be righteous so he can judge rebellious angels and send them all into the Lake of Fire. So Satan immediately takes up the challenge to reveal what is inside of Job. In doing so, Satan hopes to reveal what is secretly inside of God.

And he immediately begins to tear up Job's life. He is certain he can expose even righteous Job for the fraud he believes him to be. Once his "outwardly" good life is destroyed, Job will curse God; "skin for skin," as the demon crudely says. From Satan's perspective it would prove that there is nothing to loyalty, or to giving expecting nothing in return. Every man has his price and there is no such thing as a selfless love.

In his twisted brain there is no true love on earth or for that matter even in heaven. Satan operates on what men call the law of reciprocity; 'You scratch my back, and I will scratch yours.' Satan is convinced that once God withdraws his protection, God's little "pet" Job will emerge as not really being righteous. Once the blessing is gone Job will curse God. And Satan secretly hopes that the God whose image Job bears will be shown to be the same.

That is how it works on Satan's side of things. When men follow him they become just as he is. So Satan, in his own self imposed deception, actually thinks he can prove God's motives are no more pure than his own. And why? Because Satan is motivated every day by a fear framed vendetta to escape from his eternal destiny in the Lake of Fire. To do this he tries various things. One of them is to find unrighteousness in God. If there is no such thing as a righteous love, then God is not the righteous judge he says he is, and he has no standing of superior moral stature with which to judge. So at this point in the discussion God seems to grow quiet. There is no doubt he is luring the accuser into some sort of trap and Job is the bait.

> Does Job fear God for nothing? Have you not made a hedge about him and his house and all that he has, on every side? You have blessed the work of his hands, and

his possessions have increased in the land.(Job 1:9–10, NASB)

But God's challenge to the devil illustrates three things; all important to the argument between them. Satan knows that God is more powerful than he is, and that God at times does put a hedge about those he watches over; and it seems that he is able to tell when God is doing this. But most important, by causing havoc in Job's life, Satan hopes to prove that there is no such thing as righteous love, and without that there is no such thing as a righteous being. So Satan immediately takes the bait and asks permission to destroy godly Job. Satan obviously delights in destroying honorable people.

God allows Satan to touch the things Job has and even his children, but not his life, and Satan departs to begin his malicious invasion. Soon Satan's power takes hold, and by the next day Job has lost everything, even his children are all dead. As the reports come in, Job suffers shock after horrible shock, and in the midst of such loss, Job arises, tears his garment, and proclaims; "Naked I came from my mother's womb And naked I shall return, the Lord gave and the Lord has taken away, blessed be the name of the Lord," (Job 1:21, NASB) and we, and all the host of heaven and hell, are left to wonder at such words from a man so stricken.

But Satan, not yet willing to give up, makes a second stop to speak with God. And it is at this meeting the devil makes a direct attempt on Job's life.

> Skin for skin, He cries. Yes, all that a man has he will give for his life. . . . put forth Your hand now, and touch his bone and his flesh; he will curse You to Your face.(Job 2:4–5, NASB)

So the Lord again grants permission, and this time for Satan to touch Job's body, but again draws the line at his life. Satan seems almost giddy as he will be able to prove all the good that comes from Job is because of what God has done for him. And perhaps after all that Job has endured, we might even be a bit scandalized by all the incredible unfairness this has developed into, but God's ways are higher than our ways, and this experiment is all in his control. Besides, nothing is ever lost with God, he can restore it all in a moment.

But as the experiment proceeds, all the host of heaven watching, all the angels good and evil, must discern why God has made Job a demonstration of what authentic love really is, and how tawdry is the imitation of Satan. Real love pays the price, no matter what that price becomes. God so loved the world that he gave his Son all the way to a Roman cross, at personal expense.

But Satan's imitation unfortunately prevails among human beings. Too often, when we dig down, we discover most human affection is of the wrong kind. When young lovers love, they are in a sort of rapture over the process of love, but they really love themselves. They love being in love. Human beings too often have a satanic sort of imitation love and as Satan expects they enter into relationships for what they can get. When the return is gone, so is the relationship. Even the so-called "love" between married people is most often based on the principle of getting. We give affection to gain some combination of sex, protection, and property, and when those are gone, a divorce is almost inevitable. We barter good looks or great wealth for what we call love; and thus we "love" to get things which fade quickly. God looks for the sort of love that remains unbroken when a young man returns from war, his face burned beyond description, and she stays firmly by his side. God is looking for the sort of love that continues after bankruptcy, or the loss of a child, or when one spouse falls into dementia. Often when such things intrude; marriages discover that their love was based on reciprocity, and the marriage crumbles. It is no wonder that with Satan so few actually believe a righteous love even exists. And Satan leers knowingly at such "bought and paid for" levels of affection. These he understands perfectly, and he believes all "love" is of this type.

But God is looking for something far higher, God is looking for righteousness in his relationship with us, and with each other, something which reflects himself, and not his enemy.

So Satan destroys Job's life, trying to debunk Job's kind of love for God. All the arguments you read from his so-called friends which follow in the book are really an elaboration of the same. We finally find Job in the dust with scabs all over his body, mournfully scraping his lesions with the sharp edge of a pottery shard. He has lost his wealth, his children, and now even his health, and by this time his wife is showing what she is made of. Admittedly tested to the end of her endurance, she is through with God, her love having been based to some degree upon what she could get. She finally flips out and tells Job to curse God and die. She too believes in reciprocity.

But not Job, not this amazing man Job. With a broken heart he tells her; "You speak as one of the foolish women speaks. Shall we indeed accept good from God and not adversity?"(Job 2:10, NASB) And in all this Job demonstrated to the watching angels what a selfless love is like. In a rage, watching from wherever slime hole he watches, Satan and all his evil host are left with their mouths gaping wide open, screaming in anguish. Angels have now looked into these things and they too have seen what righteous love looks like. It has been demonstrated even in the weak humanity of Job, and now the evil angels know their fate is sealed.

Since God pointed Job out for the demonstration, and since Job is only human, Job must be a poor imitation of what God is like. Job is a sinner and needs a Redeemer by his own admission. But God knew Job's incredible righteous heart; and he knew Job would come through with flying colors. Job does understand the sort of love that is selfless and true, and God his creator must be something many times better.

Nevertheless, Job in all his adversity was only a litmus conducted to show what real love is all about. If mouths are shut over Job, what a wonder will come when the real event takes place. Because another greater test would come in the future. The greater test that Job alludes to in his song. And it is the test where weak things based on love would have to contend with strong based on force. Jesus would be called to love all men in such a selfless way. And this time there would be no limits placed on his enemy. Satan would be given full power even to take his life. The righteous King of Heaven would boldly place himself into the claws of heartless power, the very teeth of his great enemy, and allow him to do his worst. Jesus could have met force with overwhelming force, but he chose the weak things of this world to overcome the strong. Not as the Almighty One, El Shaddai, with limitless power, but with the gentle love of the Passover Lamb, would Jesus set the captives free.

Selfless love would prove the righteousness of the King of Glory. While saving mankind from the results of their fall in the garden, Jesus would do something far more important. In his death he demonstrates his own character, to the angelic host, and to all that watch. The angels would finally get to see the character of Almighty God unmasked. And by the way, this is the solution to the mystery of why man. We were created to become the demonstration of God's righteousness. It was such risky business, this allowing men to fall into sin.

God never caused any of it, but God needed a fallen race to demonstrate what he is. When Jesus came to earth as a human baby he became such as we are. In choosing to be cast down to the utter weakness of this creature of flesh and bone, Jesus could expose the character of God which he could never do from within the sheath of power he has on his throne. God had truly chosen the weak things of this world to overcome the strong, and the simple things to overcome the wise. In his eternal power there was no way for God to put on a cloak of weakness and submit himself to the rampage of his enemy, but in the body of a man Jesus could manifest utter weakness.

At any moment God could have simply cast Satan into hell on the basis of pure power, but that would never have demonstrated to all the host of heaven what he is really like inside, the very purpose for creating mankind. Paul actually tells us this in Romans. God's justice requires holiness, and through man God has demonstrated his own righteousness. God needed some way to show his love and he found a way through the creation of man. The Almighty God has found a way to step out from behind his great power in order to save tiny beings of flesh and blood.

And while the heavenly host watched, Satan would be allowed to test him with all the vileness that fills the devil's demented existence. And God, with only the power of a pure heart and love would fulfill two needs. Jesus would become the innocent lamb, dying in place of sinful man. He would be the Lamb of God that John proclaimed would take away the sin of the world, but he would also become the demonstration of righteousness that he possesses beneath all that limitless power. Angels good and evil needed to look into that.

> whom God displayed publicly . . . this was to demonstrate His righteousness, . . . for the demonstration, I say, of His righteousness . . . so that He would be just and the justifier of the one who has faith in Jesus.(Rom 3: 25–26, NASB)

Calvin had been right in one sense, Jesus was a demonstration. Jesus became the demonstration of holy unselfish love. God never needed to demonstrate his hatred for sin, but he did need to show the love in his heart. So rather than the cosmic bully, pounding on human kind, making sure everyone knew about his sovereign power, he became the lifeboat lifting the entire human race toward everlasting life. The truly powerful never need to show off their power; only bullies and the insecure need to swagger.

> For while we were still helpless, at the right time Christ died for the ungodly . . . God demonstrates His own love toward us, in that while we were yet sinners Christ died for us. (Rom 5:6,8, NASB)

At the same time he pulled man back from the brink, God proved to his spirit being enemies that he has the righteous character to pass judgment. So the great answer to the greatest question of all is that God made man, who was allowed to fall, in order to have a creature to rescue. And he did this by becoming one of us, paying for our sins in his own blood, and allowing himself in weakness to demonstrate his love to all the universe. By stepping out of limitless power Jesus became what the Bible says was a little lower than the angels, and was placed into the clutches of the devil, to allow him to do what he had done to Job. In the process, as Jesus tells us, he overcame the world.

> but God has chosen the foolish things of the world to shame the wise, and . . . the weak things of the world to shame the things which are strong . . . (I Cor 1:27, NASB)

Righteous angels watched in disbelieving agony as from the cross Jesus yielded up His spirit. They wanted to charge into the fray and destroy the world that had treated Jesus this way. Perhaps they stood nearby hardly able to watch, as God the Son was put into a human tomb. And most likely they held somber vigil in silence and defeat as he lay there lifeless three days; was it even possible that the Son of God was dead, as a human being is dead, sign of Jonah, three days and three nights in the belly of the earth. Surely nothing had ever happened like this before. Somehow God lay dead in a human tomb.

So why was that forbidden tree in the garden of Eden? God has answered this question. From the very beginning mankind was designed to become the demonstration of his righteousness and his righteous love. Paul states it outright in Romans. God needed an entity of mortal flesh to demonstrate who he is to beings of eternal power and glory. It was always there in prophecy. The Son of Man would be placed on the tree like the brazen serpent in Numbers. And as he hung on the "tree" the curse is returned to the branch from whence it came. His death is a picture of the curse being put back onto that accursed tree.

I suppose that the Son of God still weeps for all the death and defilement of every human creature; the price required for the demonstration of His love and righteousness. But all was restored upon his cross where Satan put him. The Son accepted every sin, and paid there on that tree for all of it. As he declared, "It is finished."

Far from Calvin's grotesque notion that man is the object of God's wrath; man is the object of God's passionate love. God in Jesus turned himself over to the torturers to be destroyed in place of those who had committed the sin. But he would also rise to show his victory. He would rise to tell the world he was the loving sacrifice that took away the sin of the world. Jesus could have said these words of Paul's:

> I have fought the good fight, I have finished the course, I have kept the faith:(2 Tim 4:7, NASB)

Chapter 4

So What is the Gospel?

CALVINISM HAS SEVERAL IMPORTANT peculiarities in dealing with the heart of the gospel which demonstrate what John Calvin actually thought was the gospel message. But there is one teaching in particular that we must consider before we attempt to unpack his complex theology completely.

It is the Calvinist theory of the atonement blood. Calvin and Calvinists have an accountant like approach to the blood of Christ. They often tell inquirers that there is only a limited amount of saving blood available. Some of them use the literal blood that was in Christ's body for that basis, and some speak in allegorical terms, but the blood is still limited. Those who are of the elect, those tapped out for salvation in eternity past, get just enough blood to cover their sins, not one drop more, and everyone else is out of luck. How this fits with being tapped out before the world was made is never explained.

But you will often hear Calvinists say something like they cannot even conceive of the sovereign God allowing "Christ's blood to be wasted." They usually add color by saying that the sovereign Lord could never allow his blood to fall to the ground unused. This is their way of saying that if the blood had been applied to everyone, that is for all sin everywhere, then every time somebody died without Christ their share of the blood would be wasted. So the blood could not possibly be applied to everyone, as Bible evangelicals believe, and the Word of God teaches. If so, according to Calvinists, a bunch of blood has already fallen to the ground.

The other side of this is also true. Since God is sovereign any bit of His blood ought to be sufficient to force any unbeliever to become a Christian. This the essence of what sovereignty means in their minds. He saves by simply determining who is saved and who is not.

But this blood accounting idea flies only if there really is some magical amount of blood required to erase each sin, and each believer would get just what he needed for his particular set of sins. A lie may require a pint of blood, and a murder a whole gallon; the theft of a car might require a quart, and so on. Calvinists don't really ever make such weird statements, but they actually do mean such things. And they use this accounting of the blood to fortify their "Limited Atonement" theology (not everyone is saved) by telling us that there can only be a limited number of people saved because there is only a limited amount of blood to go around. Later we will cover all aspects of the TULIP of which Limited Atonement is one aspect. But according to their own definition it becomes unthinkable, actually flying against the sovereignty of God, to have wasted one drop of Christ's precious blood on anybody who is not tapped out in the elect.

Unthinkable, in two ways. Unthinkable because it is precious, and unthinkable because the sovereign God should be able to keep his blood from being wasted. They say that if Christ had shed even a thimbleful on anybody he wanted to sprinkle it on, the sovereign would get his blood's worth, and the person would be saved by the application of "Irresistible Grace." Imagine a god, they like to say, who is so weak he can't even keep people who actually got some of His blood out of hell!

So Christ's blood has some mysterious quality that seems to be in short supply and has the power to save if the right amount is applied to the sin. Of course all this is a complete confusion about the nature of the atonement. It is also central to the error which is Calvinism itself. So how does the "atonement" really work?

When Christ was lifted up he declared from the cross; "It is finished!" But what was finished? From the context of the Old Testament, especially Daniel's chapter nine, it was "the transgression." Man literally transgressed when he fell into sin in the garden. The transgression is literally the sin of the whole world, and Christ himself said it was finished. All the transgression from Adam to the end of the world was finished by the suffering of Christ on the cross. Messiah made an end to the transgression, the sins of the past from the garden, and even the sins that were yet to happen to the end of this present transgressed world. Daniel chapter nine even tells us how he would end the transgression. Messiah would be "cut off," in payment for all mankind. We must say once more, Daniel predicted through the Angel Gabriel that all transgression would be taken care of by the death of Messiah. Now Calvin to the contrary, if the transgression is paid in full for all, then new life in Christ is also pre-paid for all. Jesus wrote paid in full over all the sin of the world. That is not the same as saying all people would be saved, but all people have had their sins paid in full, the requirement to be saved. But just as you may have prepaid for your airline trip, unless you arrive, walk down the jetway and take off with the plane, you won't go anywhere.

> For as in Adam all die, so also in Christ all will be made alive.(1 Cor 15:22, NASB)

All human beings were in sin and all were destined for hell. In like manner as in the parallelism above; all in Christ are made alive. All who were destined to die and go to hell have had their debt paid in full, and are destined with Christ to live forever. But not all of them will. They have to get on board the plane. Nobody falls through the cracks, because the blood did its payment for everyone, and not one soul was lost. Nevertheless, the individual person, since he is free to make up his/her mind can as Jesus warned us; take the wide road to destruction or the narrow way to everlasting life.

SO WHAT IS THE GOSPEL?

But because I say that the door is open to everyone, Calvinists accuse people like me of being Universalists, proposing that all get saved. They believe that if this salvation was available to everyone, then everyone would get saved. Who could be so foolish as to miss out on the gospel train when it pulls away from the station? And yes how terrible that would be, and yet some will still choose the wide road that leads to destruction. The truth is Christ and Christians would actually like to be Universalists, in order that all people would go to heaven. But some do end up in hell, and that can only mean they shut the door on themselves, and refused Christ's offer.

Christ's blood takes away the sin of the world, as John the Baptist announced it would. His blood paid for the whole transgression, all sins by everyone, for all time. There never was any question about how much blood would be enough. All the transgression is paid for with all the blood because the amount of blood actually has nothing to do with it. While Jesus' blood is precious, it was his life that was required. Jesus could save hundreds of billions, or just one, and it would take the same amount of blood; all of it. The sacrifice of Christ would have been required for all men, even if there was only one who would have responded. It is the sacrifice that matters, not how much red fluid came out of his physical form.

He was not splashing a bit of blood on one person here, and a bit more on another one over there until the blood ran out. All the blood is required for every sinner. It is not the amount of the blood, but the price of the forgiveness that saves. The price was his death.

Moreover the blood does not force anybody to go to heaven. The person decides to believe and receive, and that determines where they want to spend eternity, just like father Abraham desired God and was saved. As he promised Jesus lifted up draws all men to himself from the cross, but the decision to follow him remains with the person.

For what does the Scripture say? "Abraham believed God, and it was credited to him as righteousness.(Rom 4:3, NASB)

But as many as received Him, to them He gave the right to become children of God, even to those who believe in His name.(John 1:12, NASB)

According to 1 John 2:2 the propitiation (the payment) has been made for the sins of all men. Thus all the blood has already been spent. God is not holding some of it back to apply to the lies of one, and the car theft of another. The transgression was paid in full for all the sins of all the people for all time. As he said, it was finished. Listen to Paul's words to his intern Timothy:

For the grace of God has appeared, bringing salvation to all men, . . . (Titus 2:11, NASB)

Jesus called himself the open door. In Revelation he stands next to a door and knocks, asking to come inside. Whatever the metaphor actually encompasses, a doorway is an access, an access to everyone who wants to pass through the opening he asks us to go through. Since the transgression is finished, God in Christ has opened a door into eternal life. It is the way, the one way where salvation is offered to everyone who wants to pass through. He himself is the Open Door, and a "Door" so open that no man can close it again. Jesus commanded us to go through him and take the narrow way that leads to everlasting life. But he also warned us that the vast majority would decide to take the wide road that leads to everlasting destruction. And yes, Jesus would rather be a Universalist if men would all decide to go his way. Because Jesus loves all those he created, every last one of us.

Behold, I [Jesus] stand at the door and knock; if anyone hears My voice and opens the door, I will come in to him and will dine with him, and he with Me, . . . (Rev 3:20, NASB)

But the Calvinist, knowing better than Jesus, immediately shouts his objection claiming that choosing one road, one door, one way, is a work, and men cannot work for their own salvation. Calvinists seem to have a hard time deciding what a gift is, though I sincerely doubt any of them misunderstand the concept of packages under the Christmas tree. Under their teaching picking up your package and unwrapping it would constitute doing something to earn your gift! Believing John Calvin instead of Jesus Christ, they cry error, they cry works, they cry legalism. They tell us that we are contributing to our own salvation by making the choice of the road we follow, the very road described by Scripture which leads into the arms of the waiting Savior.

> Enter by the narrow gate; for the way for the gate is wide, and the way is broad that leads to destruction, and many are those who enter by it. For the gate is small, and the way is narrow that leads to life, and few are those who find it.(Mat 7:13-14, NASB)

In the Calvinist mindset they believe it impossible for anyone to refuse so good an offer as the one Jesus makes, and they say this while they themselves are refusing to accept the offer. So somehow, and they don't know how, Jesus words about choosing open doors and narrow ways cannot be true. You just cannot choose to go to Christ and not be working for your own salvation, or so Calvinists say. Apparently for salvation to be completely without works the Savior must unexpectedly tap you out in some esoteric spirit world before time began. But Calvinists are right, there is a "chosen" people. In ancient Israel God did choose a people to be his own. God looked down and found Abraham. Israel is the chosen people of the Old Testament.

> After these things the word of the Lord came to Abram in a vision, saying, "Do not fear, Abram, I am a shield to you; your reward shall be very great." . . . And He took him outside and said, "Now look toward the heavens, and count the stars, if you are able to count them." And He said to him, "So shall your descendants be." Then he believed in the Lord; and he reckoned it to him as righteousness.(Gen 15:1,5-6m NASB)

Israel is the only people the Bible actually describes as a chosen race. Those who came forth from Abraham were to be put into the service of God. But like present day Calvinists, many of them came to think of this choosing as an automatic entitlement for heaven. They began to believe they were going to glory on the basis of their choosing. But not only did many of them end up in hell, but a few like Korah fell directly through a crack into the earth when the ground opened up.

> and He himself is the propitiation for our sins; and not
> for ours only, but also for those of the whole world.
> (1 John 2:2, NASB)

Christ paid the price for all men, and yet he tells us that some will still choose the wide road that goes to their own destruction. It is the narrow way and the open door and the road is open to anyone willing to go. Judas felt deep remorse, and though he too was one of the chosen, and chosen again by Christ himself to be an apostle, yet he went to his own place, and that place was not heaven. Many others will do the same. They hear the gospel which has the power to save, and yet they will go to their own place, as Judas finally did.

Calvinists refuse the gospel, reject the open door, and forsake the narrow way. They do not listen for the knocking of the Lord, and without one Bible verse to support them choose to believe their Calvinist mantra in the face of the plain teaching of the Word of God. They have been told that their regeneration (the new life in Christ) happened before the world was made. At their baby baptism they are told they shall be part of an "elect" that they cannot find in the Bible, and are depending on for everlasting life. Surely they are blind to the plain gospel that has been saving everyone since the Savior went to the cross.

> that if you confess with your mouth Jesus as Lord, and
> believe in your heart that God raised him from the dead,
> you will be saved; for with the heart a person believes,
> resulting in righteousness, and with the mouth he con-
> fesses, resulting in salvation. For the Scripture says,

'Whoever believes in Him will not be disappointed.
(Rom 10:9–11, NASB)

The Lamb slain is sufficient for all men. Because, as John said, he is "the Lamb that takes away the sin of the world."

Chapter 5

Eklektos as the Elect?

In the 300's Jerome, a Bishop in Rome, was commissioned to translate the Word of God from Hebrew and Greek into Latin, the language of the priesthood in the Roman Catholic Church. Jerome produced the old *Latin Vulgate* around 383 AD and it has remained the basic Bible for Roman Catholicism ever since. It was the first Bible translated into what is called the *vulgar* tongue, Latin for the language of the common man.

Much later the *Vulgate* became one of the primary sources for the most important English translation which was translated in the 1600's, the authorized or *King James Bible*. Erasmus, another Catholic monk, used original documents in making what is now called the *Textus Receptus,* a Greek text of the Bible, but his manuscripts were somewhat skimpy so he was often forced to resort back to Jerome's Latin version to fill in the blanks. Withal, it is clear that Jerome had a marked impact on all the Bibles of the western world and especially the Bible used by those who speak English.

Jerome was a capable translator but not an experienced one, and it is the nature of the translation process to accumulate errors at the best of times. He was commissioned by the Pope to bring back those who were scattering from the Catholic umbrella, so that many views of classic Catholic thinking crept into the translation, many of which have trickled into the English Bible where they have gained a home that still taints many modern translations with Catholic meanings. He was doing something fairly new, something a few even thought wrong to do in the first place. Some still argued that the Bible ought never to be read in anything but its' original Greek and Hebrew languages.

Thankfully that debate seems to have been long resolved, and there are translations in myriads of languages today. Even then, Jerome's effort was far from the first translation. Some seven hundred years prior, in Alexandria North Africa, the *Septuagint*, (a name that reflects the seventy venerated Jewish scholars who did the translation) had already translated the ancient Hebrew of the Old Testament into Greek. Young Jewish scholars in Alexandria had largely lost the ability to read and write Hebrew. There had been several other attempts at translation, but Jerome began the first serious attempt to bring the whole Bible, both Old and New Testaments, into a new language which most people could read.

And he made every effort to work with the best copies of both the Old and New Testaments, and he did possess documents of some antiquity. But this was all before the printing press and every copy of the Bible, including his own in Latin, were written by hand, and no doubt the hand written manuscripts he was using also contained copying mistakes which accumulate from human error. Moreover, Jerome as a dedicated Roman Catholic, in an age in which Catholic thought and practice were not just the leading persuasion but the only form of Christianity, was dedicated to seeing that the peasant world conformed to the Catholic church. It was natural that he should think this way but his bias toward Catholic tradition was bound to come out of his manuscript. This was a world where the very word "Catholic" meant the Universal Church. As a result several awkward sacred "cows" of translation, some of which still haven't been taken out persist into our modern translations; English and otherwise.

Moving from one language to another is a very precise and exhausting pursuit, and the challenge for the translator is to infuse the translation with the original intent of the writer. But it is almost impossible to choose the perfect word every time. And Jerome has become notorious for starting the battle over the Greek word *metanoia,* which in English means simply "to change one's mind," but in the Catholic world of Jerome, where doing penance after confession to a priest was so important, Jerome couldn't have converts merely "changing their minds" about anything especially Christ. They would have to recite the rosary hundreds of times, climb stairways on bloody knees, and do other penance before they would be considered cleansed by their Catholicism. So instead of the English words "confession to God" which would have done very well, the word "repentance," took hold and has never relinquished itself, even into modern English translations. Instead of merely changing our minds, as Paul tells us in his epistles by confessing our sins and giving them up to God, we are still trying to force upon converts grave feelings of deep remorse as in repentance. There are at least twenty-six places in the New Testament where the Greek *metanoia* is still translated "repent."

Another such debate which is more germane to Calvinism, has surrounded the Greek word *eklektos.* According to the seventy authors of the *Septuagint,* who settled many questions of meaning long before Jerome, *eklektos* was always used to replace any Hebrew word meaning something of great value or excellence, or something of choice quality like a choice crispy apple. The *Septuagint* scholars were all bilingual, having great facility with both Hebrew and Greek, and they were a committee of the best translators of their day. With the Seventy the exact definition of the Greek word *eklektos* had been carefully established. In fact they give us insight into the meanings of many Hebrew words by their translation into Greek at a time well before Christ.

A very good example might be; "with the pure, you show yourself pure" Psalm 18:26. Something of great purity has great value. So the seventy translators of the *Septuagint* chose *eklektos* to substitute for "pure" or "righteous" as it is in some English translations such as the NASB version of this verse. They decided that something excellent would also be described in English as pure or righteous. In the *Septuagint* this psalm is translated using *eklektos.*

An expression of quality has little to do with being picked out or chosen from out of a group. One could envision a quality thing being picked over something mediocre but the two things, the being picked versus the being valuable, are not the same. So *eklektos* properly translated has little or nothing to do with choosing something, but everything to do with something of quality. In another example, the Seventy Jewish translators also carefully translated the Hebrew word *bachir,* (which means excellent) into *eklektos.* Something which was *bachir* or excellent, in Hebrew, would be called *eklektos,* in Greek.

Whether Jerome knew about any of this in his day is all conjecture. But we do know in the translation of *eklektos* into Latin he picked out the Latin for "chosen" rather than "excellent" or "choice," and chosen in Latin would become his most used meaning. He thus fell into a direct contradiction with the translation team of the *Septuagint,* who hundreds of years prior would translate *eklektos* into something "special," or "excellent" or even "choice," if they had been using English. As we have already repeated several times, *eklektos* is never something chosen or picked out from other things, but it is always used to describe something with intrinsic value. Gold would be eklektos because gold is something with intrinsic value, gold is always *eklektos.* But Jerome picked words that in English would lead to the word "chosen" rather than "choice." In Hebrew a *bachir* soldier would be a warrior with great ability to fight, whether he would be chosen to go to the battle or not. He would be a choice man and not necessarily a chosen one.

Thus we assert that one of the most important mistranslations Jerome introduced into the Bible was the transition from what in English should be "choice" to what in English is now often but not always translated "chosen." It is actually tragic that only a few translators over the years have wanted to correct the problem because the word "chosen" or even "election" had gotten so deeply associated with certain verses, though they never added clarity to the meaning. Most of them did not even see it as a problem because the insertion of chosen into the text didn't traumatize the meaning very much. Even in Vines Greek Dictionary, though "choice" not "chosen" is listed as the first synonym in English for *eklektos,* and its cognate noun and verb are both listed as something of quality, "chosen" is also specified, though it is third. Nevertheless because of Jerome most places in the New Testament English Bible where *eklektos* appears, the word "chosen" is inserted into the text. There are however some contrary uses, which follow the proper rules of interpretation.

While many grammarians regard this as a minor problem, we want to emphasize the English word "choice" is a very different word than "chosen." They are not synonymous in the least. The two words do not conjugate together in any verb form and except for similarity in spelling being chosen is nothing like something being choice; one is an action word, the other a condition of being. They are not cognates because they mean very different things.

But Jerome actually clouded the issue by adding an additional twist when he introduced his own Latin. For example when he translated the famous verse 1 Peter 2:9, which often appears in English as " . . . you are a chosen race . . . "from his original guidance it has long been rendered with "chosen" but he increased the problem in his own Latin. Here he translated the Greek *eklektos* into the Latin as *genus electum* which actually does mean "chosen elect," when put back into English. So relying on Jerome's Latin, the proper translation into English would then be, "You are a chosen elect race . . . ," and that is exactly how it has come down to us. As it appears in the *Vulgate* Jerome's Latin clearly got into the way with: *Vos autem genus electum . . . "* Which means: 'You are a chosen elect race', and there is no question that if Jerome's translation is correct, then Calvin is a little more vindicated, because much of his doctrine of election comes from verses just like these.

But Peter, under the inspiration of the Holy Spirit, actually wrote: *hurneis de genos eklektos* in his native Greek, and that really means. "you are of the choicest (or finest) people," a far cry from being picked out. Once again *eklektos* is expressing value, rather than imparting election. The actual text with this Greek word *eklektos* always imparts a very different meaning to the verse than the one most translations have promoted to the general user since the time of Jerome. Generations have read, loved and memorized a good number of verses with this mistranslation in them. So at this late point in time, which ought to be used? The tradition of Jerome's personal word preference, or the accurate Holy Spirit's speaking through Peter the Apostle? Actually this writer is not really sure.

But here is the rub. Calvinists have always used the Jerome spin on the words "chosen" or "election" so that the Bible seems to have one factor on the Calvinist side of the debate. From the very beginning some in the church have taught sovereign election because of this major switch in meaning so very prominent in the English New Testament. It appears over 20 times in the Epistles and has cognates that also are used in the same way. As we stated, the translation "chosen" has become so traditional, many have memorized the texts using these wrong words and are committed to the sound of them in English.

Nevertheless, Jesus himself presents to us a very different view of salvation in the parable of the soils, which appear most clearly in Matthew thirteen. Unlike Peter and Paul, Jesus never uses the word *eklektos* in this parable, but he does describe the "choice" soil, the person who is choice in his sight, and the reader will note that there is no person in the parable who is chosen over the others.

There are four kinds of people who are randomly seeded with the Word of God. Four types of soil, four metaphors for the hearts of persons who receive the gospel. In another thing of interest to our discussion, there has been no tapping out from all eternity past. These are all people born into this world, people who are not yet saved. Apparently all four are able to receive the "seed," the Word of God, which seems strange since each of them ought to be Totally Depraved and unable to be saved, according to John Calvin. Each soil seems to have some inherent quality that either makes it ready or not ready to receive the seed in the present hour. The seed is scattered like seed has been scattered from the beginning of time. Some lands on the hard packed ground, metaphor for the person who has no interest in spiritual things, and the seed can't even penetrate the ground (the heart) of this sort of ground, and the agents of Satan eat the seed before it can germinate. A died in the wool Calvinist would no doubt claim that this soil represented the Totally Depraved though it only represents one fourth of those who have the seed fall on them. But even here Jesus states that the seed didn't germinate, not that the seed "couldn't" germinate.

Then some of the seed falls on rocky ground, where the soil is thin. This is the sort of person who emotionally grasps for the truth without thinking about consequences. These seeds germinate and grow up rapidly but they have no root. The seed in the rocky soil usually dies in the first few days because it was only an emotional decision.

And there is the weedy soil which is full of the cares of this world. And such a person is weighed down with so many problems and sins. Such soil cannot produce much fruit because the world is in the way, and its usefulness is choked out. Interestingly enough, Jesus does not say that this soil did not germinate the truth, just that it does not produce much fruit and is not choice.

But in the midst of all these poor soils some finally falls on "choice" soil that produces a crop. Some produce less than the others, but this rich soil always produces something. God would like to see a good harvest out of every soil into which the seed falls, but he is less worried about quantity than quality. God is concerned about reality. Even those who can only produce the thirtyfold belong to the choice converts to the Lord. The Lord is showing us what a choice Christian is like. A choice believer produces a crop for God's Kingdom. God's precious souls produce from the fruit of the Spirit. The Word goes into them and they grow it out with much increase like good soil and produce a good crop.

Notice that none of the four soils was chosen, and every one of them received the same treatment. Every soil had the same seed falling upon it, but there was a dramatically different result. None of the four was a soil picked by the sovereign will of God in days previous to its existence because the "choice" soil only shows up after the seed is placed inside. And choice believers produce fruit, a crop, the seed is planted in their hearts and it grows up into more. There is nothing here about some mythical mystical existence before the world was made, where the "elect" are tapped out and regenerated before they are born. And there is no Total Depravity where the inquirer is unable to even read the Bible, or receive the seed of the Word. It is the Bible which is planted inside and yields the fruit.

Calvin hammered a mistranslation by Jerome into a whole theology. Christians, he said are a race of men "chosen by God before the world was made." They are the elect, a very small group that through no action they take on their own behalf become believers. When they are born, they don't even know they are the elect. That all this has no bearing on what Jesus said should be very evident by this point.

Finally, to add to all this confusion, the very English word "elect," even sounds a bit like *eklektos*. But the only connection between the two words is a transliteration based only on the sound. Calvinists have always used Jerome's translation to buttress their own ideas of election, but it is based on a faulty foundation. The concept of "choice" instead of "chosen" fits much better into the context of most of the New Testament. And sometimes, simply because the context will allow nothing else, the English word "chosen" is abandoned, even though it is still *eklektos* on which the versed is based. The correct translation "choice" works in every case, even here where "chosen" cannot possibly replace *eklektos* and make any sense.

> And coming to Him as to a living stone, rejected by men, but "choice" [eklektos] and precious in the sight of God, . . . Behold I lay in Zion a "choice" [eklektos] stone, a precious corner stone, and he who believes in Him shall not be disappointed. . (1 Pet 2:4–6, NASB)

Vines Dictionary often gives examples of the word being defined as used in a verse. The first biblical example actually taken from Vines, Matthew 22:14 "Many are called but few are chosen," actually means little or nothing as written. How does it follow that someone called is not already chosen? Why would you be called if you weren't already chosen? It is redundant. It would be far better to render it, "Many are called but few of those are of the best quality." This verse is in the context of a parable where those attending a wedding have literally been dragged in off the streets and alleyways. It also makes sense in light of the soils. God is going to save many but only a few really produce the fruit of the Spirit.

And in another of Vine's references, Luke 23:35 " . . . let Him save Himself if this is the Christ of God, His Chosen One." But Jesus is the only Son of God, the precious Lamb. And unless there are a number of such Sons to pick from, or some other person could do what he does, he can't be "the chosen one". Chosen presupposes there are others to choose from. But there is no other like he is. He alone is the "choice" one. So when the thieves on the cross are hurling insults against Jesus, they are actually saying; 'this is the Christ of God, His only Choice One.'

When Joshua chose leaders for his army, the Hebrew word *behar* appears in the Old Testament, meaning only the best were used. He had to pick the strongest, the smartest, and the most brave to lead his men into battle. So yes he chose them, but it was because of their intrinsic quality, rather than some other criteria which led Joshua to choose. Obviously they were chosen because they were choice, and not choice because they were chosen. They were chosen because they were the best not chosen because they were chosen.

These were the choice young men of Israel. The seventy of the *Septuagint* translation team in correctly communicating Hebrew into Greek once again used the word *eklektos* for this part of the Word of God. The best scholars of their time, fluent in both Greek and Hebrew, said the Greek word that best communicated *behar* was *eklektos*. The best word in the entire Greek lexicon for a Hebrew word that meant "most excellent" was *eklektos*.

So even from this brief overview we understand that the word "chosen" when it is used in place of *eklektos,* and often used to buttress the Calvinist theory of election, gives the wrong impression. Those who are in Christ are not especially "chosen." God wants to save every man, woman, and child, but they may be "choice," depending on the sort of "soil" that they are when God's seed falls on them.

Chapter 6

Syllogism: The Logic of Calvinism

CALVINISTS HAVE AN INTELLECTUAL sort of faith and love to argue theological concepts, especially with those who are not Calvinists. They consider themselves the Biblically elite for accepting John Calvin's views of theology and think it only a matter of time before all Christians accept his theories. Right this minute many large denominations like the Southern Baptists are in enormous wrestling matches to determine their future statement of faith, though there are slight variations of Calvinism even among its' proponents. However, there is one issue on which all Calvinists agree. They absolutely deny the ability of someone who is non-elect to invite Christ to come into his life and be changed by his own decision. They reject the right of men and women to be saved in the here and now. They never say so in print, where they could be quoted, but in fact they deny such a thing as even a possibility.

While a few of them would say such a way to God is merely improbable because of what they read in the Bible, they actually do not believe in conversions where people simply confess their sins and invite the Lord Jesus Christ into their lives. Calvin himself called such an event an emotional decision that would quickly fade away.

To make this even more confusing, they appear to be doing traditional evangelism and sometimes even join into citywide campaigns, such as those Billy Graham used to conduct. This is something that may confuse Bible Christians. Savvy Bible Christians know Calvinists don't believe in "on the spot" conversion, and yet they are often found doing more "outreaches" and evangelistic campaigns than most of the rest who claim to be regular Christians. And their campaigns have the same look and feel of what is seen in other places.

But Christian beware, such Calvinists have not changed their opinion about calling people to convert to Christ. They are still convinced the "elect" are saved only by being chosen by God himself; and most say they have received new life in Christ even before the world was made. They are saying in effect that they were saved before they were born.

So is their evangelism just window dressing? Perhaps it is for some, but for the majority there is a kind of logic in doing this. Regular Christians wonder why they bother preaching the gospel to people if their eternal destiny is already set. Are Calvinists not really so different than ordinary evangelicals? Are we mistaken about the motive and goals of Reform churches? Can somebody walk into a Reform church, hear the gospel, and go to heaven? Most Calvinists would answer in the affirmative, but they mean something different than the Bible Christian every time.

According to Calvin people come into the world already saved, or they can never be saved. So why do Calvinists do evangelism? Reform churches often issue altar calls, and many bring in evangelists; but it must be understood that the role of the evangelist is quite different in a Reform church. The call is not to get people to make a decision for Christ but to separate people they regard as sheep from the goats, the "chosen" from the general population. The evangelist is trying to locate those who are elect, but don't yet know they are part of Christ's so-called chosen few. The assumption is that those who will respond are mostly part of the elect; especially if they come from a Reformed church. The un-elect, if they respond at all, will quickly fall away, and leave the elect to gather like gold in the bottom of the pan. Because the very first principle of Calvinism is the concept of "Total Depravity," the T in TULIP.

We have already mentioned this several times in passing, but what exactly do Calvinists mean when they invoke "Total Depravity"? Traditional evangelical Christians often heave a sigh of relief when they hear about this Total Depravity teaching among Calvinists. They finally think they have stumbled onto something over which they can agree. Calvinists may be wrong on many issues but at least they understand the lost condition of man. A moniker like Total Depravity seems to fit very well, and oftentimes ordinary Christians will call themselves one point Calvinists on the basis of Total Depravity. But the Bible Christian is warned to examine this more closely.

Because such Christians would be wrong. They do not have even Total Depravity in common with Calvinists. It is not the amount of sin, or even the pervasive control of sin that makes the non-elect Totally Depraved. All people who were not sovereignty elected are part of the Totally Depraved, even those who hypothetically now might be professing Christ. They might even say that you, an ordinary Christian are Totally Depraved, but since you cling to Christ you just don't know it yet. (If you really are of the "elect" you will eventually see the light and become a Calvinist.) Calvinists claim that many ordinary Christians are really Totally Depraved and they await the moment that you will abandon Christ and admit it.

The un-elect for Calvinists don't just reject Christ, they are not even able to be saved. No preaching of the Gospel, no tract, and not even the formal study of the Bible will ever avail for such people, because they lack the regeneration that comes before they are born. (Note that Calvinists tell us that "regeneration," which is new life in Christ, happens before such things as belief and faith.) But "regeneration" is the very substance of salvation. Salvation is new life in Christ. To get new life is to be saved. So here the cart has gotten in front of the horse, and none other than their greatest hero Spurgeon warned them about this years ago. But Calvinists have never been terribly concerned.

What traditional Christians need to see clearly is that nothing in Calvinism is backed up in Scripture, though Calvinists themselves believe otherwise, and will fight to the mat over this one issue. Calvinism is a man made religion from the pen of John Calvin and at best only gives a side long glace to the Word of God.

Because of their lack of Bible understanding, contradictions with the Word of God abound. In the Calvinist world they get very intellectual and call them antinomies, and Calvinists love to debate over their antinomies. Theologians write whole books about antinomies. But the contradictions they find with the Bible nearly always vanish when Calvin is taken out of the mix. And yes, there are real antinomies, such as Christ being fully God and fully man at the same time. But a true antinomy can always be described, though it can't be rationally explained in human logic. Calvinism has many contradictions with the Bible, but they are not easy to explain, thus they are true contradictions and not antinomies at all. Calvinists deal with them as they deal with all things that confuse; they are placed into the hidden file in the Godhead. They cannot be explained or even easily described, so they are not real antinomies but since they are "according to the pleasure of his will," they are hidden in the counsels of the Godhead from the prying eyes of man.

According to Calvinist teaching you were either saved from before the world, or you are never going to be saved at all. If you happened to pop into this world, the child of unbelievers, you were probably already relegated to hell, and you have no chance to ask Christ to forgive your sins. But remember what Jesus taught to Nicodemus one very interesting and illuminating night. Jesus said that Nicodemus could be born again.

> Jesus answered and said to him, 'Truly, truly, I say to you, unless one is born again, he cannot see the kingdom of God.' Nicodemus said to Him, "How can a man be born when he is old? He cannot enter a second time into his mother's womb and be born can he?"

> Jesus answered, . . . as Moses lifted up the serpent in
> the wilderness, even so must the Son of Man be lifted up;
> that whosoever believes in Him should not perish, but
> have eternal life. For God did not send the Son into the
> world to judge the world, but that the world should be
> saved through Him.(John 3:5-17, NASB)

So Jesus told Nicodemus, who was one of the chosen in Israel, a Pharisee, a member of the Sanhedrin, one who Jesus even
referred to as the teacher of Israel, that he must be born again.
But Calvinists traditionally decry calling seekers to the front of a
meeting to be saved in the way of traditional evangelists because
they feel it gives the inquirer a false hope. And they have actually
come to abhor the name of the man who invented this method,
Charles Finney, of Adams county, New York. Strangely enough
Finney began his Christian life as part of a Reformed Presbyterian
church. But he left to become a traveling evangelist and in the process invented what he called the "anxious seat." Inquirers would
come forward and take their place in one of the seats awaiting the
evangelist to pray with them for salvation.

Thus it was Finney who began what over the years has become a veritable stampede to the front of a meeting. Even Spurgeon was criticized for throwing out the net to those he liked to
say were being "elected on site" by God. Nevertheless, rock ribbed
Calvinists are certain that the altar call is a works related heresy,
something Paul prohibits in his epistle of Ephesians. They believe
that a mere response to God by simply agreeing that he or she is
a sinner in need of being saved is the same as working your way
to heaven, and they cite the verse below. They make the case that
in the Reformed Faith God "saves" without so much as a human
nod and thus they call themselves the Gospel of Grace, or the Doc-
trines of Grace, as opposed to what they say is a gospel of works in
traditional Christianity.

Calvinists become apoplectic over this one issue. Asking
Christ into your heart is, they say, utter heresy. Salvation must
come from the sovereignty of God, acting without so much as

personal agreement, otherwise you have contributed to your own redemption something prohibited by the Word of God.

> For by grace you have been saved through faith; and not of yourselves, it is the gift of God; not as a result of works, so that no one may boast . . . (Eph 2:8–9, NASB)

The Calvinist disdain for all forms of salvation by personal invitation is the product of the "T" in their acronym TULIP. As the reader has probably surmised by this point, this letter stands for "Total Depravity."

Calvinism places the Totally Depraved unbeliever outside the blood of Christ, even outside the atonement. Such a teaching locks most of the human race into hell from birth. It seems that God put most of mankind into the world to send them to everlasting torment. And Total Depravity is the main concept of Calvinism. Even more than all the debate we have over predestination and the rest of their TULIP, Total Depravity is the key concept of the whole super structure upon which the house of Calvin depends. It is not a side issue nor is it in agreement with Bible Christianity. Total Depravity is where Calvin departs from the faith once delivered to the saints. This is the bottom line which separates Calvinism into what I believe to be a cult religion. Apparently Calvinists have never read Isaiah below.

> "Come now, and let us reason together," Says the Lord, Though your sins are as scarlet, They will be as white as snow; Though they are red like crimson, They will be like wool" (Isa 1:18, NASB)

> If we confess our sins, He is faithful and righteous to forgive us our sins and to cleanse us from all unrighteousness. If we say we have not sinned, we make Him a liar and His word is not in us.(1 John 1:9, NASB)

Such verses as these are the expression of God's fervent grace toward man in an everlasting covenant of love toward his creation. And compared to the forgiveness which comes down from the cross as expressed in these and many other verses, Total Depravity sits like the monstrosity it is, and serves to punctuate the distance between grace and condemnation. Such is the distance between Calvinism and Christianity.

Saving the ordinary person, which happens every time a sinner is born again in Christianity, is actually impossible in Calvinism. It would be the ruination of Calvinism. Though salvation is the everyday substance of Bible Christianity. Christianity rests upon salvation. Calvinism rests upon condemnation. Christianity rests upon good news. We don't have to go to hell. Total Depravity is the bad news message of Calvinism, and yes, most of us do go to hell. We must see that Calvinism is not Christianity.

Calvinism actually finds its' origin in a coupling of five logical links in the TULIP chain. The chain is put together by a system of human logic called the syllogism. Each link is dependent upon the one before it, and the enlightened Calvinist will rightly say there is no such thing as a two or three point Calvinist. To break any link in the chain is to break the whole. A person is either a five point Calvinist or he is no real Calvinist at all.

But to introduce the logic of Calvinism we begin with an explanation of the "syllogism," the type of logic Calvin used by intention or intuition to come to the full array of TULIP. This logic form entails a first premise, which is supposed to be a statement of truth, and a second premise that supposedly follows from the first. Then it provides some sort of conclusion from the two statements. This works as an IF THEN statement in a computer program where it is under numeric control. But in human logic it has fallen out of use. Because among all formal logic forms the syllogism is most prone to go wrong. If either of the two premises are incorrect or do not follow logically one from the other, the resultant conclusion will also be wrong.

For example, if my first premise says that; 'All reptiles have muscles,' which is a truism, but follow that with premise two saying; 'I have muscles,' which is also true, but has no direct bearing on the first statement, then my resultant conclusion will be in error. Since reptiles have muscles, and I have muscles, I must be a reptile, which all but a few of my strongest enemies would probably call error. Weak as this form of logic is; from Total Depravity onward, the TULIP of Calvinism works in a chain of syllogisms. Bear in mind that the original declaration of Total Depravity sets the stage and that already is a statement of Biblical error. I will list each in the series of tables which follow:

Table 1. The "U" in TULIP:

UNCONDITIONAL ELECTION
Premise 1: Total Depravity (inability to come to Christ)
Premise 2: Some are still saved
Conclusion: God saved them by his own intervention.

Once the doctrine of Total Depravity – the inability to come to Christ, is accepted, then the theologian looks about for another method for people to be saved. Since it is obvious that some do get saved, how is it possible for those who are unable to come to Christ to still come to Christ? The only way is for God himself to force it to happen. So enter the doctrine of "Unconditional Election," or it could better be called the doctrine of "salvation forced upon people." Nobody can be saved unless God forces it upon them.

But the question that ought to be asked after so startling a doctrine is promoted; is where in the Scriptures can this doctrine of "Unconditional Election" be found or even surmised? Where in the Bible is salvation forced on anyone? The doctrine of the Trinity is not written out in Scripture either, but it is not difficult to discern such a teaching from what is in the text. At his baptism Jesus is present, the one being immersed, the Holy Spirit descends as a dove, and the Father speaks from the sky. This demonstrates the three part nature of God. But such a doctrine as Unconditional Election cannot even be elicited from other parts of the Word of God. It is entirely forced by the underlying syllogism. Calvinists insist that Unconditional Election must be in the Bible because the premise of Total Depravity demands it be there.

Nobody knows exactly when "new life" (regeneration) comes into the life of the elected person, but it doesn't matter. What matters is that God regenerates a few "chosen" ones, perhaps to show that not everyone goes to hell, and he does so prior to their birth. All is done, according to Calvinist jargon, to defend the sovereignty, and what seems to be the fragile sovereignty, of the Almighty God himself.

Under this rubric elected people are already regenerated at birth despite the fact that "new life," the "new birth," actually is salvation, as even Spurgeon admitted. Calvinists believe that faith in Christ will follow, but for what reason is never explained. Perhaps it is needed to fit the biblical narrative better. That every Bible verse which speaks about salvation says that faith precedes regeneration never seems to dawn on these people.

> Truly, truly, I say to you, he who hears My word, and believes Him who sent Me, has eternal life, and does not come into judgment, but has passed out of death into life. (John 5:24, NASB)

It was none other than the Prince of Preachers, Spurgeon, regardless of how much he proclaimed himself a Calvinist who understood such a peculiarity as regeneration prior to birth was already salvation. Anyone having the "new life," or the "regeneration," that comes with Christ, is already saved. From his preaching Spurgeon knew that he had to coach a man to have faith to open the door before any person could invite Christ come in and be resident in his life. The Holy Spirit woos us, but the person is never violated, and must open the door of his heart by confession of his sins and a personal invitation to God.

> To as many as received Him gave He the right to be called the children of God. (John 1:12, NASB)

The next link in the chain of Calvinist logic is the "L," standing for "Limited Atonement."

Table 2. The "L" in TULIP

LIMITED ATONEMENT
Premise 1: Unconditional Election
Premise 2: Not everyone is saved.
Conclusion: By design God does not save everyone.

Triggered by Unconditional Election, a cascade of logical steps must inevitably follow in this theology and Calvin followed them to their bitter end. But most Christians are rightly shocked by the "L" in TULIP. Bible Christians are taught that the blood of Christ was sufficient to deliver all sinners from hell and into salvation. But this is the normal world where sinners accept Christ as their personal Savior. In Calvin's world where God himself chooses a select few, there seems to be no moral reason for not saving everyone. (What have embryos done wrong, anyway?).

The natural conclusion is that God must be withholding salvation from most of the human race. Here the god of Calvinism emerges as some sort of cosmic bully who picks some and ignores others without any reason except some unexplained fear of Universalism. Calvin's theology makes God into a bad actor who would prefer to damn the vast majority of people to a hell forever than to rescue them. Such is Limited Atonement. Apparently there is not enough blood to go around.

Next in the TULIP is the "I" Irresistible Grace. Grace applied to specific sinners by force. But to force anything upon anyone is no longer grace. Therefore this combination of words is an oxymoron, two words which cannot really go together. Grace by definition is something given without coercion, God's grace is his love bestowed upon mankind without getting anything in return. When Calvin's associates like Beza invented the combination, "Irresistible Grace" they created an impossibility, an oxymoron. If grace is forced, it is no longer grace at all. Here then is the syllogism for Irresistible Grace.

Table 3. Irresistible Grace, the "I" in TULIP

Irresistible Grace
Premise 1: Limited Atonement
Premise 2: A few are kept out of hell.
Conclusion: Salvation forced on those few.

And the final letter in the acronym is the "P," or "Perseverance of the Saints," meaning that salvation once assigned is permanent, and cannot be lost. Many if not most Christians believe that once applied salvation is never lost. Eternal life is not very eternal if you can lose it every so often. But here Christians rejoice, actually believing that here they have found a doctrine in Calvinism that they can agree with. Often Biblical Christians will say they are two point Calvinists because they believe in Total Depravity and this Perseverance of the Saints. But unfortunately neither can be supported in Scripture the way Calvinists define them.

Calvinists never have assurance they are going to heaven because they never know for sure they are part of the elect. Since Calvinists have no assurance which can only be shown to them out of the pages of the Word of God they attempt to "persist" by the legalistic proving of their own election over and over again.

Table 4. Perseverance of the Saints the "P" in TULIP.

PERSEVERANCE OF THE SAINTS
Premise 1: Irresistible Grace
Premise 2: Election is an automatic trip to heaven.
Conclusion: You cannot lose your salvation.

SPECIFIC VERSES WHICH CONTRADICT THE TULIP HERESY:

1. **Total Depravity** (The inability for salvation for a person who was not chosen by God.)

   Therefore putting aside all filthiness and all that remains of wickedness, in humility receive the word implanted, which is able to save your souls.(Jas 1:21, NASB)

   Come now, and let us reason together," Says the Lord, "Though your sins are as scarlet, They will be white as snow; Though they are red like crimson, They will be like wool. (Isa 1:18, NASB)

2. **Unconditional Election** (Only God chooses who goes to heaven, and individuals cannot even accept the free gift of salvation Jesus offers, because in doing so, they have gone into a works doctrine.)

   Opening his mouth, Peter said; "I most certainly understand now that God is not one to show partiality, but in every nation the man who fears Him and does what is right is welcome to Him.(Acts 10:34–35, NASB)

For this is the will of My Father, that everyone who beholds the Son and believes in Him will have eternal life, and I Myself will raise him up on the last day.(John 6:40, NASB)

3. *Limited Atonement* (Christ's Blood does not cover the sins for all people. Some just must go on to hell.)

And He Himself is the propitiation for our sins; and not for ours only, but also for those of the whole world.(I John 2:2, NASB)

4. *Irresistible Grace* (Those saved have no part in the decision, because it is forced on them.)

Jerusalem, Jerusalem, who kills the prophets and stones those who are sent to her! How often I wanted to gather your children together, the way a hen gathers her chicks under her wings, and you were unwilling.(Matt 23:37, NASB)

You men who are stiff-necked and uncircumcised in heart and are always resisting the Holy Spirit; you are doing just as your fathers did.(Acts 7:51, NASB)

5. *Perseverance of the Saints* (You will never have any assurance of salvation. Therefore you must prove you are of the elect by working hard for God.)

My sheep hear My voice, and I know them, and they follow Me; and I give eternal life to them, and they will never perish; and no one is able to snatch them out of My hand. My Father, who has given them to Me, is greater than all; and no one is able to snatch them out of the Father's hand.(John 10:27–29, NASB)

As we said, the syllogism is one of the weakest types of logic because it is prone to be misused. Both premises must be correct, and the second must actually follow from the first. The syllogism has failed Calvinism in the construction of TULIP. But rather than following the clear hermeneutic of the Word of God, Calvin chose to cling to his first premise of Total Depravity. After that Calvinism becomes nothing more than a return to bondage in legalism, and can offer no security in Christ. It is the Galatian heresy; having begun with faith such men thought they could be made perfect in the law.

> It was for freedom that Christ set us free; therefore keep standing firm and do not be subject again to a yoke of slavery.(Gal 5:1, NASB)

Chapter 7

Boiler Plate Calvinism

THREE SMALL SECTIONS OF Scripture: Ephesians Chapter One (Eph 1), Romans Chapter Nine (Rom 9), and 2 Thessalonians chapter two, the thirteenth verse (2 Thes 2:13), have become the boiler plate proofs of Calvinism. It is said by Calvinists themselves that if you cannot prove Calvinism in these three chapters, you cannot prove Calvinism at all. "If it ain't there, it ain't anywhere," as the old preachers used to say.

We begin with a detailed look in the first chapter of Ephesians.

> just as He chose us in Him before the foundation of the world, that we would be Holy and blameless before Him. In love He predestined us to adoption as sons through Jesus Christ to Himself, according to the kind intention of His will. (Eph 1:4–6, NASB)

Fervent Calvinists believe that God's sovereign predestination couldn't be better presented than with these verses. There is sovereign predestination plain as day; so say such ardent Calvinists as Sproul and Piper. The only way into heaven is to be "lucky," one of the chosen ones God predestined to adoption, according to the pleasure of His secret will, before time began. Those who are true Christians are predestined to be the chosen, and they are the only ones going to heaven.

And here the word "predestined" actually comes from the Greek root word "proorizo" which does indeed mean predestined in English, unlike Jerome's use of "eklektos," which we have seen in a previous chapter. So finally we have come to a verse which actually does tell us we are predestined for something. But predestined for what? The verse says nothing about salvation. It does not say that we are predestined to be saved. It says we are predestined to be adopted. The question is who is going to be adopted, by whom, and why?

This whole chapter is addressed to "the saints" who are at Ephesus. We get this from the introduction to the book here at the start of chapter one. These "saints" are not the statues in a Roman Catholic cathedral, these saints are the believers, the believers in Ephesus. Everyone who is saved is a saint, according to the Word of God. It is the truth regardless of what Rome has to say on the subject. So this is addressed to saved people in Ephesus, and these people are not being predestined for salvation, they are being predestined for adoption. They are those Paul calls faithful to Christ Jesus because they are already "saints."

So here Paul is either saying that the saints are predestined to become saints, which makes no sense, or they are predestined to become something else. And this verse does predict something wonderful is coming to the believer. It tells us that once we are saved we shall become adopted into the household of God!

Perhaps that may not seem very special because we have been exposed to this verse without giving it much thought. But it is wonderful because God didn't have to make us part of his own household. We could have happily been the servants, and the grounds keepers, and even the accountants and builders working for the King of Kings and Lord of Lords forever. But instead we are going to be welcomed into the very household of God! And that is something new and quite incredible. Christians knew they would go to heaven, but they didn't know that they would become something like ken to Jesus the Son of God, in his relationship to the

Father! It is almost too much to wrap the mind around, and is new and spectacular. Christians are not being predestined to salvation because they are already saved. Paul is saying that their salvation will qualify them to become sons and daughters in the family of God. As sons and daughters they will be conformed to Christ! Believers are not just going to live forever, though that alone would be stupendous, they are destined to actually find a place in the home of the living God. Verse eighteen is the crescendo and sums up this wonderful chapter:

> I pray that the eyes of your heart may be enlightened, so that you may know what is the hope of His calling, what are the riches of the glory of His inheritance in the saints, and the surpassing greatness of His power toward us who believe . . . (Eph 1:18–19, NASB)

God could have allowed the saved to stay forever in the bliss of heaven, and that alone would have been wonderful. But God always does exceedingly above everything that the human mind can even conceive. So God has chosen to allow those washed in the blood to become part of His own household. This as a subsequent to being saved, and it is an awesome and wonderful discovery. In heaven we will have an inheritance as sons and daughters of the King of Kings. We heard the gospel, we believed the gospel, and Christ came into our lives. Once in Christ we were predestined to be conformed to him, and incredibly to inherit what Christ inherits:

> . . . you also, after listening to the message of truth, the gospel of your salvation –having also believed, you were sealed in Him with the Holy Spirit of promise, who is given as a pledge of our inheritance . . . (Eph 1:13–14, NASB)

But leaving Ephesians, we move on into 2 Thessalonians, and there we encounter the verse:

> But we should always give thanks to God for you, brethren beloved by the Lord, because God has chosen you from the beginning for salvation through sanctification

by the Spirit and faith in the truth. It was for this He
called you through our gospel, that you may gain the
glory of our Lord Jesus Christ.(2 Thes 2:13–14, NASB)

The context of this verse is the coming of the "lawless one,"
the Antichrist is coming.

that is, the one whose coming is in accord with the activ-
ity of Satan, with all power and signs and false wonders,
and with all the deception of wickedness for those who
perish, because they did not receive the love of the truth
so as to be saved. For this reason God will send upon
them a deluding influence so that they will believe what
is false, in order that they may be judged who did not
believe the truth, . . . (2 Thes 2:9–12 (NASB)

The Apostle is simply telling these people that he is giving
thanks to God because they won't fall for the lie. God has chosen
to save them from the lie through their sanctification in the truth
of God. Sanctification is not salvation from hell. Sanctification is
to be retained by the knowledge of the truth. These believers will
not believe the lie, a lie so powerful that God says he has sent it out
himself, as a kind of test for those who know the truth.

But these in Thessalonica will not be detoured by even the
deluding influence that God will send. God has chosen to sanctify
them in the truth. They are the church in Thessalonica and God
has chosen that they should not believe the lie. In fact God chooses
to do that for all who are his. So this is not a Calvinist verse in any
way at all. It is merely Paul telling the Thessalonians that they will
not be allowed to become deceived by the lie that will come on the
world when Antichrist comes onto the scene.

And finally, saving what Calvinists consider their best for last,
we plunge into Romans chapter nine, the most "Calvinist of all
Calvinist" sections in the Bible or so Calvinists themselves like to
say.

Just as it is written, Jacob I loved, but Esau I hated.(Rom
9:13, NASB)

Calvinists feel they have a trifecta in this chapter. They have three horses in this race that build on each other, right here in Romans nine, and it gives them a victory that horsemen at a racetrack would call a trifecta.

It begins with the verse above and Jacob as loved and received; apparently from the womb, while Esau is hated and rejected from the same. By implication Jacob goes to heaven and God sends Esau directly into hell, though we do observe that no mention of heaven or hell are in these verses anywhere. Still the point Calvinists are trying to make is that God arbitrarily does what he does, for no discernable reason available to the human mind. God just does such things because he is sovereign. And in doing so he somehow demonstrates his justified sovereign wrath toward sin. It is all, as Calvinists love to say; hidden in the pleasure of the counsel of his secret will .

Then for the second of the three, they cite the potter in verse 21:

> Or does not the potter have a right over the clay, to make from the same lump one vessel for honorable use, and another for common use? What if God, although willing to demonstrate His wrath and to make His power known, endured with much patience vessels of wrath prepared for destruction? (Rom 9:21–22, NASB)

By which the Calvinist means to demonstrate that God fashions people like Jacob for honorable use and Esau for a lesser or common one, in order to demonstrate His wrath and sovereignty; Esau they will tell you was "prepared for destruction" by the sovereign will of God before the world was made.

And finally number three of the trifecta:

> For the Scripture says to Pharaoh, 'For this very purpose I raised you up, to demonstrate My power in you, and that My name might be proclaimed throughout the whole earth. So then He has mercy on whole He desires, and He hardens whom He desires.(Rom 9:17–18, NASB)

And by this point the non-Calvinist, who is lacking in his Bible, is feeling threatened. Calvinists feel they have this section of Scripture so wired together that ordinary exegetes will shy away from even going here.

So what do Biblical Christians do with this apparent hatred for Esau, with the potter creating such vessels destined for destruction? And what do we do with Pharaoh, who was hardened against the truth, predestined to go to hell; as we said, the trifecta of Calvinism?

As always we begin by looking at the context. Because it is still true that a text without a context is a pretext. One very large reason Romans was written by Paul was to present the Jewish Messiah to his own people, who are also Paul's people, Israel. And while the Reformed do not often speak about them, Israel is the chosen people And that is why he takes them up in the first place. In verses 1-4 of Romans 9 Paul sets the stage for what he is going to be saying next.

> For I could wish that I myself were accursed, separated
> from Christ for the sake of my brethren, my kinsmen ac-
> cording to the flesh, who are Israelites . . . (Rom 9:3-4,
> NASB)

Paul's main purpose in writing Romans is to get his own people, God's chosen people, into heaven by changing their minds about Jesus. He would have been willing to suffer for all eternity in hell if his own people would just come to Christ. And such a statement is already anathema to the idea of the chosen getting tapped out before birth, and how interesting is the thought that such a chosen people are in danger of hell in the first place. I don't imagine Calvin could ever come to such a conclusion about the people he believed were his chosen. According to Calvin their very election is an election to heaven. Calvin certainly wasn't telling all the world that his chosen elect could die and go to hell. How could that happen if they were regenerated even before they were born? And Calvin certainly was not like Paul, willing to go to hell on behalf of his people!

So for a first principle, we understand that being chosen is not the same as being saved.

Jesus actually chose twelve Apostles for service to himself and one of those, Judas Iscariot he chose, he called a devil. Thus in both choosings; as Jesus' disciples, and as part of the nation of Israel, the chosen were chosen for service and not salvation. God often chooses a man or a people to serve His purposes. Therefore being chosen is not a "get out of jail free" card, as Calvin assumes in regard to his own apparently imagined "elect." So even if there is some proper use of the word elect in the New Testament, it does not necessarily entitle the bearer to a free trip to heaven. According to the Bible, most of these who were actually chosen Jews ended up in hell because they did not receive the Savior God had provided for them.

> who are Israelites, to whom belongs the adoption as sons, and the glory and the covenants and the giving of the Law and the Temple service and the promises, . . . from whom is Christ according to the flesh, who is over all, God blessed forever. Amen.(Rom 3:5, NASB)

Not only is this chapter about service and not salvation, Romans chapter 9 is about Israel the truly chosen, and not Calvin's so-called "elect." But let us enter into the Reform hermeneutic and consider how they are using these verses.

Calvinists begin their arguments using a very dishonest formulation in Romans 9:13, " . . . Esau I have hated.." If Calvinists don't know that this verse has nothing whatever to do with the original Jacob and Esau themselves, they ought to know this. But Calvinists act very ignorant or very dishonest right out of the chute in this chapter of Romans nine. "God hated Esau, and loved Jacob." as though this was about these two young men themselves. Of course nothing could be further from the truth. Reading Genesis, where this reference comes from, a book Paul makes allusion to often because all Jews knew this story very well, Rebekah had the beginnings of two nations in her body, the nation of Esau and the nation of Jacob, who seemed at war within her womb.

> The Lord said to her, "Two nations are in your womb;
> And two peoples will be separated from your body; And
> one people shall be stronger than the other; And the
> older shall serve the younger.(Gen 25:23, NASB)

Calvinists hope that you will not read Romans through the context of Genesis because you will quickly discover that God is not saying anything about hating Esau personally. And he certainly wasn't declaring that Esau would be condemned from the womb as Calvinists often spin this thing. Rather it was the people of Jacob instead of his older brother who would inherit the promise of God. So God was not condemning Esau, but he was preferring Jacob. God was placing Esau in exactly the position of all the rest of the un-chosen peoples of the earth. Yes, he was rejecting the first born from receiving the heavenly birthright to become the chosen of God, but he was not sending anyone into hell, at least not in these verses.

In Romans God is speaking to two peoples, not two brothers. And even though Paul uses the sort of language Jesus uses when he says we must "hate" our parents, as used in this context it is a word of contrast. You must love God so much that in contrast it seems that you hate your parents. It's a call to put obedience for God over even your loving obedience to your parents, though the Commandment to honor them persists. And Calvinists know all this too, or they ought to. God is speaking to two nations and commending Jacob for his service, and it actually is painful to this writer that Calvinists are so biblically ignorant or downright deceptive as to continue using this old saw.

And even though Israel was chosen, not every Jew would go to heaven, and by the same token, not every child of Esau would go to hell. Actually I think it is a near certainty they do know about this, and are running a bit of a scam. Still they need this hatred for Esau in order to pursue their arguments from this chapter. For in the very next section Paul does remind anyone reading Romans that God is sovereign, much to the delight of Calvinists, but not in the way they expect to be made happy. They expect us to conclude that God sovereignty judges some and keeps others, as in the way they explain Jacob and Esau.

> ... I will have mercy on whom I have mercy, and I will have compassion on whom I have compassion. (Rom 9:15, NASB)

Instead this is a statement about God being God. And yes God is sovereign, but he is not capricious. Even in the case of Jacob and Esau God had reason to be angry with Esau who loved his own stomach more than the promise given to his grandfather Abraham.

But remember, in context God is speaking to Israel. And all he is telling them is that they cannot depend on their "election" for everlasting life, the very opposite conclusion that Calvinists want you to come to. God is simply pointing out that he is God. He is free to pardon and punish whomever he desires to pardon or punish, and why is that so earth shaking? So this verse is really saying nothing about Calvinism. What is stated is simply a truism about of the nature of God. God will judge the quick and the dead, and there is no power on earth that can resist him.

And why does he take the time to remind Israel? Because he is preaching to a smug people who have the idea that since they are the chosen people they no longer have to obey him like other people do. They think God will always be on their side, but God is reminding them that he will still pass judgment over them based on their faith and not their lineage. So this verse really has little to do with the Calvinist argument one way or the other. All that the potter is about is comprised in learning how to obey God.

Paul has already stated he would go to hell for them, if that might help, because he fears most of them are going there. But he has no power to stop them. And in the midst of such teaching God reminds everyone that he is the potter. It is an apt metaphor because God still has all of us on his wheel. Like a potter making various vessels for his service in which some come out good and some not as good, though the Bible uses the word "common," meaning a common use which may not always imply a bad use.

God is in the business of fashioning lives, all lives. And as Paul points out, some pots are made for common use, and they may be more important than those made for food or beauty. On one hand God may want to create a vase filled with flowers, but on the other a commode filled with something else. And which of these two pots is more important? Sometimes God needs a pot for an important job that is not appreciated. Some pots get used for food, some become beautiful plates, and some end up catching human waste as it goes into the sewer. Some pots hold beautiful bouquets, and some are used to wash dishes. In this verse the potter fashions some to be wonderful, and some to be useful, which may be more important than mere beauty. But nowhere does this verse go beyond the analogy and state that the potter delights in smashing his pots just to prove he can do it. But why does God fashion his pots? Doe he do it for salvation? Never, he does it for his use in the household of God. Some serve the table and some serve the sewer but all have their place in serving the body of Christ.

No human potter controls every detail of how a particular pot is used or abused. God fashions the pots and while he always knows how their lives are going to turn out, he does not destroy just to demonstrate their imperfections. He may intervene to re-direct, but he does not control. Some may fall on the concrete and shatter, and some might actually be beautiful vases and get used for inferior purposes, but he fashions the pots to be just as they should be regardless of how they end up being used. No potter tries to make inferior pots, and God is the master potter. He fashions them knowing what they will become, but in no place are we told he controls their use or their destiny.

There is no predestination here, and certainly no Calvinism which demands that the human race be created just to be destroyed, apparently demonstrating his sovereign power to destroy the pots he just made. He is a potter forming a pot to be the best it can be, but since the "pots" are alive and not cooperating, some of them come out wrong.

Like the potter God has been molding the nation of Israel. And while they remain in exile he used Egypt as a tool on the spinning mud, and he is here telling us why. Pharaoh became a tool in his hand. God put Pharaoh into a high human throne to demonstrate His own power, and to fashion his people to follow him. This is not a universal statement applying to all men everywhere. This is a statement about a particular monarch raised up as a tool in the hand of the great potter, in order for the potter to mold His people. It is for Israel that he fashions a tool called Pharaoh, just as any potter uses knives and knobs and other sorts of tools, tools that very often he fashions for a particular use.

In the process God destroys Pharaoh. Not because he predestined Pharaoh to destruction and hell, but because Pharaoh hardened himself like bad clay on the potter's wheel. And even this is not predestination; it is discipline. God called Pharaoh to obey him numerous times and every time Pharaoh balked, as God knew he would. As with Adam God never caused him to disobey; he chose that route for himself and God simply hardened him in his way. It is an old cliché but the same heat that can melt a heart can also harden the clay.

As we have stated many times before, God does know everything but he does not cause everything. It is Pharaoh that brought the discipline of the Lord into his life and while that probably does have application to everyone, it does not mean God picks out individuals to send them to hell. God worked with Pharaoh as an antagonist for the good of Israel. But Pharaoh was not picked out before he was born to be against God. He chose to be against God.

Eighteen times the Book of Exodus tells us that Pharaoh hardened himself until he became a worthless tool that was no longer useful and needed to be destroyed. God helped in the process only after he had hardened himself, a warning to all of us who disobey the Lord. Eventually God's patience ran out and he acted, forcing Pharaoh to go to his own place much as Judas went to his. God had already given Pharaoh ample chance to change his mind and he simply refused to do so. There was no predestination to destruction here. This is not Calvinism but rather an old fashioned lesson in obedience, as Paul intended it to be.

So the potter demonstrates how God works in the life of Israel, and there are lessons for us in the church as well. God did not orchestrate what happened there for some mysterious purpose in order to demonstrate his sovereignty, though we must be honest enough to say he could have. But he chose to work with Pharaoh. God attempted to get Pharaoh to comply and live, but Pharaoh would not and so God was forced to destroy a pot that was not good.

Reading this chapter in context as it ought to be read, Romans nine is not a proof text for Calvinism. It has little to do with the template Calvinists try to ram into it. We discover that Paul is not even addressing the Church except as an observer. He is trying to convince Israel to follow Christ. And while these verses do show a true chosen people; the chosen people is Israel. If it was about Calvinists it might be a bit shocking to find out that most of these "chosen" are not going to heaven. But this is not about Calvinists. It is about Israelites.

Finally, the potter and the clay explains what happened with the hardening of Pharaoh. The potter was working him and he hardened into a vessel useful to God by rising up against Israel, but God is never stopped. He could have been useful by rising up to help. God can make vessels which are with him, and those which appear to be against him but they never thwart him. And there is nothing uniquely Calvinistic about the discipline of the Lord.

And these are the best Scriptural cases Calvinism has. When read in context they utterly fail the Calvinist use of them and we quickly watch the Calvinist exegesis evaporate. None of these verses demonstrate any part of TULIP, nor do they show predestination. If these are boiler plate, the whole scheme can be easily shown to be outside the Word of God.

Chapter 8

Strange Doctrines of Grace— History of Calvinism

I've got a little list—I've got a little list
... They'd none of em be missed—they'd none of em be missed.

—THE LORD HIGH EXECUTIONER. [1]

IN THE YEAR 1536 AD, only 40 years after Columbus made his world changing trip to the New World, and about twenty years after Martin Luther nailed his 95 *theses* to the door of Wittenberg Church, Geneva city father William Farrell convinced an obscure French monk by the name of John Calvin (1509-1564) to come and lead the Reformation in his city of Geneva. Jean Couvin, in his native French had been influenced by the writings of Luther and had recently published what became his own life's work, *The Institutes of the Christian Religion*. A work which would forever change the future of Christianity, but which hardly made a scratch at the time it appeared.

When Farrell found Calvin he was a young priest, twenty-two years old, just out of university, a young man given to writing

---

1. Gilbert, W.C. & Sir William Sullivan, *The Mikado*, Act I, Part V

large tombs and he had just completed this very large systematic theology. If Farrell had not discovered him acting as a clerk in his local Catholic diocese, Calvin would have remained an obscure monk, one of thousands in Europe at that time. Joining the Reformation what he had published was finally identified as being anti-Catholic, and Calvin was put on the watch list of rebellious reformers, and dismissed from his job with the church. Young Couvin had not as yet taken his own vows which might have sealed him into Catholic service, and probably would have kept his name from ever impacting anyone again. But as the Reformation had changed his mind about the Roman Catholic Church, he would never take those Catholic orders. But if Farrell had not discovered him he might have ended up another pauper on the street. According to his biographers, Calvin had already moved farther away from traditional Catholic doctrine than Luther ever would, and he expressed his Reformed views in what eventually swelled to three large volumes. But we wonder about his real separation from Catholicism since he was so enamored of Augustine, who is still one of the great defenders of Catholic theology. We really are skeptical of Calvin's great objection to all things Catholic then or now. But he did publish, and this alone was a gargantuan task. Imagine, taking on such a project at an such an early age. But he fought it through to completion and most Calvinists still call him one of the greatest exegetes of all times. In these books he proposed his own version of the gospel and some say his own religion, heavily influenced by reading Augustine, who he regarded as the dean of the early churchmen. In fact he quotes Augustine slavishly, at least 200 times in the three large volumes of his *Institutes*.

But Farrell convinced him to come to Geneva in Switzerland, then known as a licentious and colorful city, in the midst of which Calvin began propagating his religion with puritanical fervor and immediately became a controversial character. Almost from the start he was accused of trying to ram his Reformed faith down the throats of a ribald city. It wasn't long before the town counsel began to spar with him over petty issues such as how to run the communion. In response Calvin, never one to go along with compromise, quickly became mired down in minor squabbles with the same people who had so recently invited him in.

Calvin preferred unleavened bread as one of the elements of the Communion, and the city fathers wanted bread with leaven, mostly because they were trying to assert leadership over the young firebrand. In reality such things as what went into the communion were of little importance to the politicos of the city council, but enormously important to Calvin. But the attempt to control the young Reformer failed, and a petty spirit being displayed on all sides came to a head one Sunday morning when according to Calvin the spiritual "mood" inside the service was so diminished that he refused to administer the communion at all. This was something unheard of in reformation Protestantism. What had been a minor skirmish now became a serious difference, and the council sent both Calvin and Ferrell packing. Enraged the city council met and fired both men and sent them back into Austria. Afterward they announced that religion such as young Calvin's was too radical and declared his emotional state somewhat dangerous. How much anguish they would have spared the world had they stuck to this decision forever.

Unfortunately Calvin only remained three years in nearby Austria, preaching his brand of reformation theology in a French church while the City of Geneva was becoming ever more filled with contention, straying ever farther from what was regarded as proper Christianity. Rival factions within the city threatened to destroy what comity was remaining and public immorality was flourishing. The city fathers feared they had made a terrible mistake and reluctantly invited Calvin and Farrell back to take charge of the religious education of the people in Geneva.

As for Calvin, determined not to end up in the same state of confusion, and never one to back away from using political power when he had the advantage, made certain demands on the council effectively making him dictator in Geneva. He would become like the Lord High Executioner of the Gilbert and Sullivan play, the *Mikado*. "I've got a little list . . . "

The city was going to become the showcase of the Reformation, regardless of what the people wanted. To Calvinists today this was like heaven on earth, a high water mark to strive for. To most of the world, Geneva, Switzerland would become one of the most totalitarian nightmares in the history of man. It would be an experiment in how the contract of society works under the control of someone who was fanatical to see his own version of religion at work.

And from the outside it all looked so promising. All government would be run according to the principles of the Bible, at least in theory. But most historians not enamored with Calvin's dogmatic fanaticism, tell us that it never became the paradise people envisioned, even for the church going people of the city. Geneva became an autocracy under the control of one fanatical person and resulted in the complete loss of freedom for everyone in the city. It became the classic experiment in how awful legalistic religion can become. Calvin made himself first citizen, even ruling over such personal details as dress, diet, and church attendance. Homes were regularly inspected to determine such details as the number of shoes one might possess. Missing church could get you fined, imprisoned, or even burned at the stake. Calvin was made a special member of the Council and would often overturn their decisions with his all powerful veto of anything he didn't like, and that was almost anything they enacted which he hadn't suggested. Eventually the Council was so cowed that when Calvin was ill, and he was often ill, they moved their meetings into his bedroom. They had to make sure they didn't overstep some boundary he had set.

Like any modern potentate they grew to fear his every pronouncement. We often think of the French Revolution as being the most terrible example of totalitarian power, but Calvin's Geneva rivaled it. Nearly fifty burnings at the stake followed, and many other types of execution from beheading to drowning were happening on a daily basis. The aphorism about power corrupting always seems to come true. When a town turned over all control into the hands of this autocrat, with rapidly growing intensity liberty went out the window. As things progressed, Calvin became ever more violent and vindictive.

Tyrant over the city of Geneva from 1541 to his death in 1564, he created a showcase for religious legalism. Once again, since the forbidden tree in the Garden, righteousness has never been produced by the use of behavior modification even under the terror of the rack. It is true that we must train up a child in the way he should go, but we cannot assert such control over adults. Godliness comes through a changed heart and the residence of the Holy Spirit in a life. Nevertheless Geneva is still held up by advocates of the Reformed faith as the model to which they might yet attain. Apparently like most dictatorships it was crime free and kept this way by the ever watchful eye of the local authorities eager to please Calvin's intense self righteousness.

Many of today's Calvinists applaud him for his tireless determination to make Geneva a godly paradise. But history is not so kind; calling him a petulant madman who would tolerate no deviation from his edicts. Depending on whichever biographer you read, Geneva was either under a reign of terror, or the very cloak room for the gates of heaven.

But it is hard to find anyone who really liked Calvin himself. Neither side thinks that Calvin was an especially kind and benevolent man. Geneva was not only dangerous because of Calvin's religious intolerance, but it became a nightmare of submission to Calvin's own cutting temperament. There is nothing more oppressive than an inquisitor who is determined to make all people into the mold he has determined for them. Calvin was one of these and his "paradise" was enforced by banishments, beheadings, and burnings. Sometimes it was more humane to be executed than banished. Many widows of Calvin's purges died on the cold streets with their children trying to find food and housing.

And Calvin never seemed able to change his mind about anything. Not many in reaching the autumn of their lives still hold to the details of what they believed in impetuous youth, but Calvin never wavered. Later in life he wrote a catechism (a series of instructions in religion) for the city based totally on his original writings. In this catechism he even remembered some of the sore spots he had suffered with the town fathers on such trivia as the administration of the Communion, church attendance, and even proper clothing.

Human kindness was not his forte. During his three years exile in Austria, Calvin, lacking any thoughts of romance in his life, was set up by his friends with a widow, a lady by the name of Idelette de Bure. And according to all reports there was at least some affection in this marriage put together more for appearance than anything else. Calvin took Idelette as wife, but from his point of view she was a heretic, an Anabaptist, a person who did not believe in infant sprinkling. Later Calvin would burn people at the stake for less. Idelette had two boys of her own and served as Calvin's wife for nine years, finally dying in 1549, leaving Calvin alone. Idelette and Calvin were never able to produce any children together, something which never seems to have bothered any of Calvin's biographers nor Calvin himself in the least.

After his return as the dictator, Calvin and his allies began to pull hard on the levers of autocracy. Many religious violations were punished as capital crimes, and often by fire. Secular crimes were considered of a lesser level and received punishments from the city ranging from shunning to beheading. Many were banished out of their homes and into the street. And such crimes would not have exacted a capital penalty except that it left people exposed to a grinding poverty and homelessness which usually ended their lives. Many women and their children were cruelly left out in the cold in this way.

One critic of Calvin, Dr. Jacques Gruet, a famous scholar in his own right, simply disagreed with Calvin on theological grounds, which might have gotten him into trouble eventually. But he had the temerity to post a sign listing his complaints on Calvin's pulpit. For this the poor man was tortured until he confessed to many terrible crimes, decapitated, and burned with his theology books, while his wife and family were forced to watch. Afterward the city council burned her house, leaving Mrs. Gruet to wander homeless and to die of exposure on the streets.

But of all the terrible things he was responsible for doing, the story of Michael Servetus, Migeal Serveto, (as his name appears in his native Spanish), reaches something of its own level. Michael, who was famous in his own right as an anatomist and is still credited for his discovery of the pulmonary (lung) circulation, had sought refuge in Geneva from agents of the Catholic Inquisition. The laws of Geneva permitted refugees from the established church to reside in the town under their protection, for an extended period of time. Migeal had been hiding from the officers of the Catholic Pope, who was trying to burn him for witchcraft, his passion being a largely misunderstood science believed to be devilish in the time of the Reformation.

Earlier he had written diatribes against papal authority, but also against the "Protestant Pope," as many were already calling John Calvin. Michael was recklessly outspoken, and a bit unstable, even insane as he was prone to rants against unseen guests in his private quarters. Michael also had the temerity to criticize Calvin on issues that were theological. Today Servetus would be called a traditional evangelical because he believed that a person must ask Christ to save him; but this was rank heresy with both Calvin and Catholicism. Even worse, Servetus didn't think the waters of infant baptism could save anyone. Nowadays these are just givens among all evangelicals, but Calvin had people burned at the stake over such questions.

And though the laws of the city declared a refugee was not to be molested; because of his extensive correspondence with Calvin, Michael had already enraged the first citizen. So the man they called the Protestant Pope went after this refugee with a vengeance.

For a person everyone thought a madman, Michael seemed to be acting fairly rationally. He knew he was walking on thin ice with Calvin in Geneva, so he entered the city in disguise, not secure in his passage through such a place, even though ruled by fellow "anti-Catholics." But he was recognized and arrested, and immediately thrown into prison. And Calvin, not amused at being made fun of by such an upstart who apparently did have a knack for being annoying, was ready to burn him at the stake.

His sequester was supposedly guaranteed by the secular laws of Geneva, but it did not work out that way. In that age any time spent in prison included the horror of such hellish instruments as the rack. And there, under the most terrible of extremities, he finally admitted to being against infant baptism, and was condemned to die in the flame.

Perhaps seeing what a violation was being committed Calvin may have been having some conscience over the matter and at this point attempted to pass the execution over to the city government. Capital punishment under the secular laws demanded decapitation, considered more humane than the terrible immolation in the fire. But Calvin's charges against him were religious and all religious execution was supposed to be by burning. Farrell logically intervened, demanding that Calvin execute the accused, his "crime" being Anabaptism, a theological violation which demanded Calvin fulfill his role as executioner for religious questions. A few days later Calvin acquiesced and Servetus was burned at the stake for being against infant baptism, something that few evangelical believers would support today.

Most are shocked by what happened to Servetus and others. Did not any of these Calvinists read the Word of God? Did not any of them understand God's great mercy? By the end of Calvin's terror, the use of the stake had become so trivial that it could follow quarrels over what bread to use on the communion plate.

Calvinists today say they have changed and deeply embrace the love of Christ, his mercy and forgiveness. But the question remains. Why should modern Calvinists be so enamored over the writings and the works of such a man? In their rush to vindicate Calvinism, Calvinists seem to have conveniently forgotten about what came from following his system; abominable crimes such as those against Servetus. Servetus wasn't the only man Calvin had murdered in the most hideous way because his ego had been bruised. Is such a man worthy of such respect as is given to him in this time? Did Calvin ever see the gates of glory? Many of us have our doubts.

And the Lord's bond-servant must not be quarrelsome but be kind to all, able to teach, patient when wronged, with gentleness correcting those who are in opposition if perhaps God may grant them repentance leading to a knowledge of the truth, and they may come to their senses and escape from the snare of the devil . . . (2 Tim 2:24–26, NASB)

Even contemporary accounts describe Calvin as a hypochondriac and emotionally a very sick man. He seems to have never been very happy with life, and determined always to have the last word in every scuffle. We wonder how could anyone have become so insecure as to demand the town counsel to meet in his own sick room? And Calvin's view of God seems to have reflected this own dour and discouraging life.

But what of this label, "Arminian," which comes from the person most consider Calvin's arch foe, Jacobus Arminius, whom Calvinists still spew forth as an epithet against anyone who dares to question their views. This title was originally given to anyone who disagreed with any part of Calvinism and remains the favorite title Reform people use to put down anyone who is not a Calvinist.

Jacobus Arminius had the misfortune of attending higher education at Calvin's school in Geneva and it made him forever infamous in the eyes of all Calvinists. Though many on both sides have never even heard his name, and it is a fact that few Arminians today even have any idea why they are called this by Calvinists. Even pastors are confused by the title thinking it describes any person who believes they can lose their salvation. What happened in Geneva to make Calvinists hate Arminius so much?

Jacobus Arminius was a son of Holland during the time Calvin was organizing and building the Swiss city of Geneva. As a lad, reading materials produced by Calvin and others, he decided to become a Calvinist even before his king adopted Calvinism for the whole country. He was fourteen at the time, and it was his greatest dream to go to Geneva to the place where the great Reformer lived and school there. But he would not get to Geneva for another six years, and by that time his hero was already gone.

But when young Arminius finally got to Geneva he quickly became a favorite and star pupil under Theodore Beza, who had taken over Calvin's role in the school. But before the first semester was completed things evidently began to unravel. There is very little information about what happened after Arminius got to the school in Geneva, and we are not even sure whether he ever finished. But we do know that things got off to a very good beginning and Beza thought him to be one of the best students to ever enter into Reform studies.

However things were not going so well on the inside for Jacobus, even as he began. As a lifelong student of the Bible Arminius' diary shows he was starting to have some doubts about what he was learning. Even before leaving Holland; he had some misgivings about things he saw in Calvinism. But for some months Arminius buried his doubts and was the over achiever of the class, and Beza had many occasions to praise his star pupil for his surpassing scholarship. But while he was becoming the star student on the outside, inside Arminius' misgivings were accumulating.

He noticed that Calvinism often fell far short of what the Bible was saying. Jacobus was a strong believer in Christ, and some of his journals and writings survive to the present. They characterize him as a respectful and caring person, but a person unwilling to compromise on truth. His writing always conveys love toward those he was debating, in contrast to the sarcasm and meanness of the followers of Calvin. And contrary to what you may hear about him from Calvinists, Arminius never threw out Calvinism altogether. But being a good "Berean," part of a group Paul congratulated for their determination to only follow truth, he found many places where Calvinism did not comport with what he was reading in the Bible.

He was nevertheless a devoted Reformer and wanted the Reformation against Catholic superstition to carry on. But he had also become disenchanted with Calvinism, and discovered that in jumping out of Catholicism those in Geneva had taken on more theological problems than they had left. Some sources say that Arminius graduated from the Calvinist school in Geneva, and others say he left early. But after his return to Holland, the Reformed Church there was wracked by questions pertaining to five areas of doctrine and theology. Often these are the same five areas that critics of Calvinist thinking speak about to this very moment. They are the same as the links in the TULIP doctrine that became the foundation for the Calvinist acronym. It became such an issue among the Dutch Reformed Churches that in 1610 they sent a formal rebuttal to Geneva to criticize Calvinist theology. This letter was called *The Remonstrance*.

The Dutch pastors, though desiring to stay in the Reformation with Calvin, had questions from the Word regarding many of the things we have brought forth in this book. In fact, it was in answering the Dutch Reformers that Calvinism really became codified into the five points they refer to as TULIP. What an irony that such a title should come from Holland.

But Jacobus and the rest of the Remonstrants were not trying to destroy Calvinism, which they still believed was the best answer the Reformation had brought, instead they were trying to remain steadfast in Christ. There is still a contingent of Reformation churches in Holland today that call themselves the Remonstrants, some 500 years later. These Dutch Remonstrants were calling for a reformation within Calvinism to make it conform to the Word of God, and it was the Calvinists which rejected their help.

But Armininism remains problematic to Bible Christians. Arminians of today actually carry along with them some false assumptions which came out of Calvinism, one reason most Bible believers should try to avoid the title, Arminian. Bible believing Christians are not Arminians no matter how many issues they hold in common. Nevertheless Calvinists still try to bestow this title upon everyone who has the audacity to question them for any reason.

Biblical Christians are probably not traditional Arminians. They might agree with many of the thoughts of Jacobus Arminius. and most of the *Remonstrance*, but Biblicists find that often Arminianism does not go far enough, and sometimes, as in the case of some modern Arminians who believe their salvation can be lost, way too far. Calvinists are aware that Biblicists of today reject the title Arminian as a slam, but apparently there is so little respect that they persist in calling all of us Arminians.

What the *Remonstrance* of 1610 did was to confront Calvinism with five areas of criticism, the five major areas in which their doctrine seems to be at odds with the Word of God. We have already shown how these five points are an integrated system of human logic known as a linking series of syllogisms. And we have demonstrated how the whole apparatus either stands or falls together as a unit. We have also shown that at the base of this structure is their view of the Fall of Man they call Total Depravity. And in knowing all this there can be no such thing as a two or three point Calvinist.

Chapter 9

Augustine's Role

CALVIN LOVED THE PATRIARCHAL church father, Saint Augustine, and called him the only one of the early church leaders he trusted. He said that the others, even those who were very early such as John's disciple Iraeneus, were arrogant to a fault because they believed in the freedom of the will of man. Throughout this small book, we have mentioned Augustine's role in Calvin's thinking, and even intimated that much of Calvin's commitment to predestination could have originated with the fatalism of Augustine's father. But now it is time to turn a light directly onto the man who inspired Calvin and find out why so many Calvinists think Augustine was the actual mind behind the religion we now call Calvinism.

Calvin's whole fascination with Augustine is a true irony if ever there was one. As the past president of Dallas Seminary, John Walvoord says, because of Calvin, it is apparent that Augustine ended up being the inspiration for both sides of the Reformation! In antiquity Augustine is known for being the great proponent of Roman Catholicism to those small groups who maintained their separation from the mother church, the very religion that Calvin set out to reform. And yet years later he is credited with being an architect of a form of Protestantism that Augustine himself would have despised. That's why many scholars claim that Augustine was the father of both sides of the Reformation.

It is quite amazing that Augustine is still referred to by leading Catholics as a doctor of the Catholic faith, and at the same time by many leading Calvinists as the patron and a master source of Calvinism. We have to admit that this is quite a feat, even though Augustine never had a thing to do with the religion that Calvin created. Calvin merely borrowed many things from reading Augustine. But among committed Calvinists Augustine is still the Man for All Seasons and is often quoted in their writings. And there are even a few Calvinists who jump Calvin altogether and attribute the whole of what they call Reform Theology to Saint Augustine.

Meanwhile to Catholics, Augustine is still one of the four major architects of the Catholic faith, and he would have been the last in line to leave Catholic religion for anything. Though touted by Calvinist leaders as a master of Bible exegesis, he was a follower of Origen's peculiar school of allegorical interpretation. Following Origen, he became a writer of stories (allegories) that he said pertained to the Scripture. He would read a passage and apply that passage through a story he concocted, as though it was the Lord speaking through parables. Through this he hoped to interpret the "essence" of the verse to the people listening. But he could come up with some wild interpretations. He once taught the sealing of the Kings (or Eastern) Gate in Jerusalem meant that Mary would stay a perpetual virgin forever. It is hard to imagine a more incredible jump in mental gymnastics than that.

Augustine was also a "replacement" theologian, believing that the church had supplanted Israel. Following him most Calvinists are replacement in their theology, believing that God has abandoned the people of Abraham. In fact one of Augustine's claims to fame is that he is attributed with the naming of Rome as the "City of God," a name that had traditionally been associated with Jerusalem. Catholics are all replacement people and believe that they are now the chosen people on the earth.

To Calvinists and Catholics the modern state of Israel is a slap in the face. Today's return of Israel to their land has a very upsetting effect on most Calvinists, in spite of the fact that every prophet of the Old Testament predicted their return in the last days. Many quite frankly hope the Islamists will drive them into the sea.

While there is no doubt St. Augustine was one of the giants of humanity in the company of those we spoke about earlier, he was mostly known in the ancient world for being a polemicist, a writer of essays condemning those who had stepped away from Rome. To his contemporaries he was known as a man with an agenda; willing to push his case through any theological roadblock and woe to those who got in his way. His acid pen pretty well destroyed another church father, Pelagius, who ended up with the reputation of being a terrible heretic to this moment. He was not. But in spite of all these intellectual faux pas, or because of them, Augustine was a force to be reckoned with in the ancient church, a character trait that Calvin admired since it was also his own.

Nevertheless Augustine's influence as a Catholic theologian cannot be overstated. He is considered one of those who created Catholic dogma as it is today. After nearly two thousand years of Catholic history; and as one of the four doctors of the Catholic faith, and a saint of the Catholic hierarchy; he holds a very high honor among Catholics. A doctor of the faith is one who is followed and studied above all others. For good or for ill, he is a pillar of support for Roman Catholic theology. But Augustine was very creative in his interpretations. Far from the model exegete Calvin and his followers deem him to be, he was in reality a terrible heretic using his imagination to bring all sorts of unbiblical confusion into the Roman Catholic Church. Most of it is still part of Catholic dogma today.

Augustine invented infant baptism. Even today Calvinists believe it reflects directly on whether someone is part of the elect of the church. Reformed people think infant baptism, the process of being dedicated into the church, is a very good indicator that such a person is part of the elect. In this Calvin owed his ancient mentor strong applause. Augustine instituted baby baptism as the only sure way to heaven. No wonder Calvin would later burn people at the stake, for abandoning this doctrine, and keeping it away from Biblical scrutiny. But Augustine was hardly the best well for Calvin to be drawing from. He began the worship of Mary as co-redemptrix with Christ, and was the first to call her the perpetual virgin. He promoted the doctrine of Purgatory, the age long cleansing by eternal penance of the souls of those who missed heaven. Worst of all he was a huge proponent of transubstantiation, the strange abuse of the Lord's Table, where the communion elements are actually converted into Jesus' own blood and body, to be worshipped and consumed during the Catholic communion. Even Calvin denied this aspect of Roman religion, though his fellow Reformer Luther, never could completely come out of it. When we think that all Moses did was strike a rock which symbolized Christ two times and it led to his death on Mount Nebo; imagine how often the priests of Catholicism crucify anew the Savior, putting him to open shame?

Manichaeism, the gnostic cult of Augustine's father, never stopped teaching a sort of fatalism that a man is locked into his fate by the position of the planets. And Augustine spent the first decade of his adult life as a strong proponent of his father's Manichaeism. It is reported that his mother's Christian faith finally overcame for him, and for a short while he was a proponent of the freedom of the will that Christianity has traditionally championed. But according to contemporary accounts, such was not to last. His biographers try to deny it, but it is more than likely that the fatalism of Augustine's early days leaked into his Christianity and remained there to influence Calvin a thousand years later.

The Bible teaches freedom of conscience and we can prove that since Jesus commands us to choose the wide road or the narrow way. So it is clear that I may choose the way to Jesus, even though I cannot lift a finger to save myself, I can allow him access, and be rewarded by going to heaven. Or I can bar him from my life and choose to go to hell. This is the way of freedom of conscience. Fatalism says I am locked into one destiny from the moment of birth, and no matter how often Calvinists deny what is so obvious, Calvinist predestination is a first cousin. So it was that Augustine became a kind of template for Calvin's theories, so much so that leading Calvinist RC Sproul goes so far as to admit the whole program came from the mind of Augustine, in the first place. And who would care to debate the origins of Calvinism with perhaps its modern day chief spokesman, RC Sproul?

Chapter 10

The Cult of Calvinism

CHRISTIANS TODAY ARE WARNED about the appearance of false prophets at the "End of the Age." People will have "itching ears" and heap up to themselves teachers who will bring in damnable heresies. On the other hand some heresies have been with us so long they feel like part of the landscape. Calvinism appears to be one of those. Calvinism has been with us so long Christians are reluctant to label it as one of those "damnable heresies," or even something just a little heterodox to the truth. Perhaps it has just been in the heart of the church for too many years and we have gotten comfortable with it being there. The human body will cover a tumor with layers of tissue, trying to keep it isolated, and that is exactly what his happened here. But if a benign tumor breaks loose and begins to metastasize it can quickly become a cancer that endangers the whole person. Calvinism in recent years has metastasized, broken out of the benign cyst which covered it for so long, and should now be called a cancer moving in the blood stream in the Body of Christ.

So let us be plain spoken about this; Calvinism is exactly parallel to other major Bible cults of today. Mormons were led astray by their capitulation to a false prophet by the name of Joseph Smith in the early 1800's, and Jehovah's Witnesses to Charles

Taze Russell in the early twentieth century, and for the past 500 years Calvinists have been deceived by a man by the name of John Calvin, whether he intended going against the Word of God or not. Most false prophets never intend to be false prophets, but they have some new insight or some new revelation and they set out to transform the Body of Christ into their view of things. This is exactly what happened with John Calvin 500 years ago.

Christians have never had any problem confronting error like Mormonism. Mormons loudly proclaimed that their "Jesus" was the brother of Lucifer and their Jesus sat down with Joseph Smith on a star named Kolob and designed planet earth to become the home of new baby gods. And Mormons make clear that there is no salvation in any other group. In like manner Jehovah's Witnesses called Jesus a "lesser god," known in Scripture as Michael the Archangel. But an angel, no matter how prominent an angel, cannot die on the cross for the sins of humankind. And while Charles Taze Russell and Judge Rutherford, who followed him, declared that the regular churches were abominations, the church has been in a battle for truth with these groups for many years.

I strongly believe Calvinism, by spinning a "Jesus" that delights in destroying the majority of the human race, without the remedy of the cross, and sending at least four fifths of all of us to hell, all to elevate his own glory, does at least as much damage to the truth as these other cult "Jesus-es" ever have? Is it not as against the Word of God for a group to proclaim there is no salvation anywhere except by being tapped out and regenerated before birth, thus teaching wrong doctrine, just like these others? Is all this not evidence that the church has entertained wolves in the garb of lambs for over five hundred years? I know we have.

In End Times verses like Matthew 24, Jesus warns Christians they will encounter deceivers, some even having a form of godliness but they will deny the power thereof. Do Calvinists not do this? They are masterful deniers of the power of God. They make the Gospel of no effect by teaching that there is no salvation to be found on earth in the Word of God, or even by clinging to Christ and his cross. Once you pass by being elected in the former world you are made ready in this world for hell and nothing else. So we can say without fear of being silenced that Calvinism is the greatest denier of the power of God of all times. While Calvinism has all the appearance of godliness, it denies the power of the message of the gospel.

Those born as the Totally Depraved are in a condition supposedly outside the blood atonement of Christ. Study of the Word, and confessing their sin will never avail for them. Such is clearly the denial of the power of the Holy Spirit, who draws all men to Christ. Calvinists do have a form of godliness, but they deny the power of God to save. These were the signs Jesus told us to look for.

It is certainly one of the greatest disconnects in all of human experience to find that the blessed Jesus, who called little children to his lap, healed the sick, and told us that the Father knows even when the sparrow falls, is also the greatest existential threat to every person alive for all eternity. And though he caused our original parents to sin he now will eternally judge most every one of us to hell for emulating this original sin? Calvinists follow a "Jesus" who is determined to glorify himself by sending most all of us to hell, while he tells ordinary people that his yoke is light and his burden is easy? It all seems so contrary to sanity.

There are at least forty verses in the New Testament which tell human beings that Christ came for all men, and to receive him by personal invitation is to be born again, just as Jesus told Nicodemus on that Passover night when they spoke. Here are just a few of these forty verses:

> For God so loved the world [*meaning the elect ?*] that He gave His only begotten Son, that whosoever [*of the elect ?*] believes in Him shall not perish, but have eternal life. (John 3:16, NASB)

> . . . he [*of the elect ?*] who hears My word, and believes Him who sent Me has eternal life . . . [*if he is of the elect ?*] (John 5:24, NASB)

> . . . and He died for all [*who are the elect ?*], . . . and rose again on their behalf [*if they are of the elect*]. (2 Cor 5:15, NASB)

> The Lord is not slow about His promise, as some count
> slowness, but is patient toward you, [*if you are of the elect
> ?*] not wishing for any [*of the elect ?*] to perish but for all
> [*the elect ?*] to come to repentance.(2 Pet 3:9, NASB)

> . . . namely Jesus, because of the suffering of death
> crowned with glory . . . so that by the grace of God He
> might taste death for everyone. [*who is of the elect ?*] (Heb
> 2:9, NASB)

Why should someone who is already of "the elect" worry
about the danger of "perishing" in John 3:16, or have to "hear the
Word" when he is already saved before this life in John 5:24, or
"have Jesus waiting for him to believe" in 2 Peter 3:9? Such verses
make no sense at all from a Calvinist perspective. But they do
make perfect sense for a race of men who must respond to the
gospel and be saved, as in traditional evangelicalism.

These verses, and many others, tell us that our Savior, who
was going away to prepare a place for us, and would return to take
us there, according to Calvinism, lied to us, and is really out to destroy us. Can such strange teaching be about the God whose cross
is the greatest demonstration ever of the love he has for us? Can it
be about the Good Shepherd who reminds us that only we "sheep"
hear his voice? Calvinism makes no sense at all in the shadow of
the New Testament. We must come to the conclusion that Calvinism is not Christian. Calvinism is another religion and that
religion is about a being that has hatred for mankind. We have all
been warned about the entity who hates mankind. He goes about
like a roaring lion seeking whom he will devour.

> Do not let your heart be troubled; believe in God, believe
> in Me. In My Father's house are many dwelling places; if
> it were not so, I would have told you; for I go to prepare
> a place for you. If I go and prepare a place for you, I will
> come again and receive you to Myself, that where I am,
> there you may be also.(John 14:1–3,NASB)

Remember the Good Samaritan? Jesus is our Good Samaritan who dirties himself and picks us up dirty and wounded lying

beside the wide road that leads to everlasting doom, and carries us to his safety, promising to return and take us to his own home.

> that if you confess with your mouth Jesus as Lord, and believe in your heart that God raised Him from the dead, you will be saved; for with the heart a person believes, resulting in righteousness, and with the mouth he confesses, resulting in salvation." (Rom 10:9-10, NASB)

> ... but these things have been written so that you may believe that Jesus is the Christ, the Son of God; and that believing you may have life in His name. (John 20:31, NASB)

We declare the Calvinist heresy to be a cult and a cult which smears the character of God and denies access into an eternity with Christ the Savior. It is inevitable that Calvinists will respond with venom, saying that what is written in this little manual is wrong and that most of what they believe about the Bible is also what we believe. Rat poison is only two percent arsenic and the rest is food. Cults try to mimic the Body of Christ. Calvin and his TULIP are now revered by millions who claim to know the Lord and some trust that he was the most orthodox Christian who ever lived. Cults rarely make their own converts choosing rather to distort the faith of those already saved or in Bible churches. Calvinism does the same. Calvinists claim to be Christians with a slight difference, but the famous historian Will Durant, who may have been one of the most brutally honest men ever would have begged to differ with you.

> We shall always find it hard to love the man who darkened the human soul with the most absurd ... conception of God in all the long ... history of ... [humankind][1]

---

1. Durant, Will, *The Reformation*, 90

Bibliography

Beale, Stephen. *7 Ways St. Jerome's Vulgate Helped to Shape the Church* (September 2020). https://catholicexchange.com/7-ways-st-jeromes-vulgate-helped-to-shape-the-church.htm.

Calvin, John, and Ford Lewis Battles. *Calvin: Institutes of the Christian Religion*, Louisville: Westminster John Knox, 2001.

Hunt, Dave. *What Love is This? Calvinism's Misrepresentation of God*. Bend, OR: The Berean Call, 2013.

More, Jacques. *The Word "Elect" Should Not Be in the Bible*. Nashville: Nelson, www.jarom.net, 1979.

Olson, C. Gordon. *Astounding New Greek Discoveries about 'Election.'* http://nebula.wsimg.com/823e8bb61e3b222edba723b371765c15?AccessKeyId=EBB3AFEAED3F744BBBAD&disposition=0&alloworigin=1.

Pentecost, J. Dwight. *Things to Come*, Findlay, OH: Dunham, 1958.

Piper, John, and Pastoral Staff. *TULIP: What We Believe about the Five Points of Calvinism: Position Paper of the Pastoral Staff*. Minneapolis: Desiring God Ministries, 1997.

Sproul, R. C. "Assurance of Salvation." In *Tabletalk, Ligonier Ministries, Inc.*, 20. November, 1989.

Thomas, Robert L. *New American Standard Exhaustive Concordance of the Bible: Including Hebrew - Aramaic and Greek Dictionaries*, 1981.

Walden, Treadwell. *The Great Meaning of Metanoia, An Undeveloped Chapter in the Life and Teaching of Christ*, Classic Reprint, 2012

Walvoord, John F. Millennial Series, *Bibliotheca Sacra*, October, 1951, 415-17.

Wilmington, H. L. *That Manuscript From Outer Space*, Nashville: Nelson, 1977

Vine, W. E., et al. *Vine's Complete Expository Dictionary of Old and New Testament Words*, Nashville: Nelson, 1985.

www.ingramcontent.com/pod-product-compliance
Lightning Source LLC
Chambersburg PA
CBHW060402090426
42734CB00011B/2225